Dynamic Worship

OTHER BOOKS BY KENNON L. CALLAHAN

Effective Church Leadership

Effective Church Finances

Giving and Stewardship in an Effective Church

Twelve Keys to an Effective Church

Twelve Keys: Audiocassette Tapes

Twelve Keys: The Leaders' Guide

Twelve Keys: The Planning Workbook

Twelve Keys: The Study Guide

Visiting in an Age of Mission

Kennon L. Callahan

Dynamic Worship

MISSION, GRACE, PRAISE, AND POWER

A Manual for Strengthening the
Worship Life of Twelve Keys
Congregations

HarperSanFrancisco
A Division of HarperCollins*Publishers*

DYNAMIC WORSHIP: *Mission, Grace, Praise, and Power*. Copyright © 1994 by Kennon L. Callahan. All rights reserved. Printed in the United States of America. No part of this book may be used or reproduced in any manner whatsoever without written permission except in the case of brief quotations embodied in critical articles and reviews. For information address HarperCollins Publishers, 10 East 53rd Street, New York, NY 10022.

FIRST EDITION

Library of Congress Cataloging-in-Publication Data:

Callahan, Kennon L.
    Dynamic worship : mission, grace, praise, and power / Kennon L. Callahan. —1st ed.
        p. cm.
ISBN 0–06–061281–9 (cloth)
1. Public worship. 2. Church renewal.   I. Title
BV15.C36 1994
264—dc20   94–1873
                                                                      CIP

94 95 96 97 98 RRD(H) 10 9 8 7 6 5 4 3 2

This edition is printed on acid-free paper that meets the American National Standards Institute Z39.48 Standard.

To Blake, Mason, and Brice, who bring joy and happiness to our lives. May their wisdom deepen, their compassion increase, their hope endure.

Kennon and Julie Callahan

Contents

Preface   ix

PART ONE: DEVELOPING A WARM
AND WINSOME SPIRIT IN WORSHIP

1. Worship for a Mission Field   3

2. A Hospitable Welcome   11

3. Leadership   17

PART TWO: DYNAMIC AND INSPIRING MUSIC

4. A Choir's Development   29

5. The Vital Role of Excellent Choir Directors   44

6. Music Possibilities   59

7. Music and Mission   70

CONTENTS

PART THREE: ADDING POWER
AND MOVEMENT TO WORSHIP

8. Worship Services with Less Inertia
and More Momentum *81*

PART FOUR: WHEN WORSHIP SERVICES
AND WORSHIP SPACES ARE COMPLEMENTARY

9. Building a Range of Worship Options *101*

10. The Comfortably Filled Sanctuary *113*

11. Developing a New Service *130*

12. The Power of the Spirit *143*

About the Author *155*

Preface

This book is for you—to strengthen your worship life. The book is for all those throughout the world who seek to worship God. Worship is one of the most precious gifts God has given us.

In healthy congregations worship is corporate and dynamic, stirring and inspiring, helpful and hopeful. It is joy and wonder, grace and peace. Through it people discover help, hope, and home.

You can study this book in four sessions. Invite the whole congregation to do this together—grassroots members, key leaders, pastor, and staff. As you study the book you will discover insights and wisdom to grow and develop your worship life.

I want to thank the thousands of congregations, choirs, choir directors, worship leaders, and pastors with whom I have shared across the years. They have contributed much to my understanding of corporate, dynamic worship.

I want to thank Julie McCoy Callahan. Her compassion, wisdom, joy, and peace have helped me greatly in this life's pilgrimage. This is the tenth work we have developed together. Her contributions have advanced each book immeasurably.

John Shopp, senior editor at Harper San Francisco, has contributed greatly to the development of this book. Indeed he has been responsible for the Twelve Keys books that are helping thousands of congregations throughout the world. The Twelve Keys literature has become one of the most widely used resources in congregations across the planet.

I want to thank Dwayne Roberts, who typed and edited the original manuscript and has contributed much to the development of the book. She is a good friend, a wise contributor, and most appreciated for her excellent work.

May this book help your congregation in worship. May the grace and peace of God be with you.

PART ONE:

Developing a Warm and Winsome Spirit in Worship

1:

Worship for a Mission Field

LIVING AND BREATHING

Living means breathing. Without breathing we cannot live. Try holding your breath. We can do it only so long. Then we are drawn to take a breath—rich, full gulps of air.

Worshiping is as natural to us as breathing. We are drawn to worship as naturally as we are drawn to our next breath. Just as breathing is central to living, worshiping is central to living.

Without worshiping we do not fully live. Just as we perish without breathing, without worshiping our lives shrivel and decay; our true selves perish.

People want to worship. When we worship, our lives are enriched. We are better able to deal with the twists and turns and the tragedies and difficulties of life. We are healthier, more confident, more assured. When we neglect worship, our lives are diminished, weakened, impoverished.

Indeed, worship is the breath of God. It is where we discover the grace of that breath and draw it in for a full life and for growth.

Christians want to share together in worship. What we do not want is to have to put up with a gathering that is dull, trivial, irrelevant, or full of doom and gloom. Instead we are drawn to worship that is corporate and dynamic, stirring and inspiring, helpful and hopeful.

There are sound and proven ways to make your congregational worship life deeper, richer, fuller, brimming with a sense of God's close presence. What is offered here and in the following chapters can help you achieve this goal.

THE GIFTS OF WORSHIP

The four gifts of corporate, dynamic worship are

- power
- community
- meaning
- hope

Worship gives *power* to our life. In worship we discover both who we are and whose we are. As we express our reverence for and praise of God, we develop our sense of identity as a child of God. As we confess our sins, we forgive ourselves and we accept God's forgiveness. We give up the grudges. We let go of the resentments. We are reconciled with others, with ourselves, and with God. In confession and reconciliation we discover a newfound integrity. We discover our strengths, gifts, and capacities—all given to us by God. As we discover confidence and assurance, we also discover a deep, abiding sense of power.

Worship builds *community* in our life. In spite of and amid the chaos and confusion that often engulf us, we find a sense of roots, place, and belonging as we share worship together. Although today many extended family clans are scattered far and wide, we still find "home" in God's family. We discover rich, full, significant relationships of community.

Worship gives *meaning* to our life. We discover what is genuinely important. The materialistic glitz and glitter, the gimmicks and the gadgets, are revealed for what they are. The flimsies of this world take their proper place. Our values center.

What is genuinely important in life becomes clearer and dearer. Life's puzzles and predicaments are seen in a new light. We may not always understand them, and, at the same time, we see more clearly the direction for our own life. We develop a sense of purpose. We know our life counts.

Worship gives *hope* to our life. We can see beyond the tragic and the terrible, the sadness and the sickness, as we discover anew the resurrection of Christ and new life in his way. We are no longer held prisoner by memory or sadness or sin. We are reborn into new life in Christ. We become the Easter people. We become the people of hope.

THE MAJOR COMPONENTS
OF A HEALTHY SERVICE

Congregational worship is corporate and dynamic, stirring and inspiring, helpful and hopeful when

- the service is warm and winsome
- the music is dynamic and inspiring
- the service has power and movement
- the services and sanctuary help the congregation reach persons in the community in mission
- the preaching expresses the character of the gospel and the quality of compassion

These are the five major components of a strong, healthy service of worship. This book is devoted to helping you with the first four. A forthcoming book will help with the fifth component of worship. Whenever these five components are richly and fully present, the worship life of a congregation thrives.

This book provides wisdom and resources, insights and practical suggestions to help you develop the worship life of your congregation. You will find the book helpful with congregations, Sunday school classes, worship and music leaders, pastors, choirs, choir directors, organists, denominational leaders, and new congregations. Invite these groupings to a thoughtful study of the book.

Gatherings for worship need not be dull, trivial, irrelevant, or doom and gloom. They can strengthen us and help our life and destiny.

Worship is corporate when we sense we are gathered as a community of faith. We discover in worship that we are the body of Christ, the family of God. There is a sense of roots, place and belonging, sharing and caring—a sense in which the community has gathered together with God in a shared and holistic way.

Worship is dynamic when people sense the stirring, moving presence of the living God in their midst. We are lifted to our best, true selves. The future is open before us. The worst of the past is forgiven. The best of the past is treasured, and the best of the present and the future is discovered. In worship at its dynamic best, we genuinely sense our lives being touched, our destinies advanced, our hopes inspired.

ENHANCING YOUR CONGREGATIONAL WORSHIP

Look prayerfully and thoughtfully at your worship services. I say "services" because many congregations in our time have more than one service of worship. Consider your services in relation to each of the five major components listed above. Discover which of these components are richly and fully present.

Think this through in relation to and in comparison with the healthy, strong congregations in your area. Do not include congregations that are unhealthy, weak, or declining. It is not helpful to consider the strengths of your worship services in relation to such congregations.

Once you have done your evaluation and comparison with only those congregations in your area that are healthy and strong, then select the three of the five major components just listed that you can constructively develop and improve in your own congregation.

Beware of that old trickster, a compulsion toward perfectionism, which may try to entice you to improve all five components. For now, focus on three of the five. Save two for a later time.

Select the three, keeping in mind these criteria:

- Your competencies
- Value to your community
- Having fun while you grow forward
- Rich promise for future mission

Competencies

Which of the three worship components best match your current competencies? You may feel especially adept at meeting new persons in a warm and engaging way. Your competency may be in music that inspires people. Perhaps your competency is in the power and movement of the service. Fine. Begin with these.

Don't try to do everything. Congregations that try to do too much in growing their worship end up doing too little. With no focus, they spread their efforts between too many different objectives.

Claim the strengths God has blessed you with and select three components that you and your congregation can best advance and improve.

Value to Your Community

As you consider which three components to improve, think through what will be of value in your community. There is a direct correlation between dynamic, shared worship and the character and quality of life in the community. The more helpful the services of worship, the healthier the life of the community.

Healthy congregations have healthy, corporate, stirring, vibrant services of worship. People's life and destiny are advanced. Families are enriched and strengthened. The congregation's outreach in mission moves forward with confidence and assurance. The character and quality of life in the community is enhanced.

Worship As Celebration

Which three of the five components would you have *fun* doing? In the New Testament, it is clear that God loves a *cheerful* giver. I believe God also loves a cheerful worshiper! Worship is not doom and gloom, whining and complaining, lamenting and bemoaning. Worship is a celebration—a time of hope and joy, wonder and grace. In this sense and in this spirit, select the three areas you would have the most fun growing forward.

Looking to the Future

Choose the three components of dynamic worship that have the most promise for your future mission. We live in a new world. It is the age of mission. We can no longer count on social conformity to deliver new persons to our worship services. Focus on the promise of your mission.

Consider prayerfully, cheerfully, and thoughtfully the persons whom God has planted all around you. Decide which three of the components listed above will help you be in the strongest position of mission with them.

Now, grow and develop the three components that are best for you. Do so with the spirit of mission rather than the spirit of a churched culture. Discover the persons you sense God is leading you to reach.

Grow the spirit of mission as you select these three components. Don't develop them primarily out of a concern to add to your membership. We are not improving worship for the purpose of church growth. More is at stake in worship than simply getting more members.

What *is* at stake as we worship is helping people advance their life and destiny in the name of Christ. Worship for the integrity of the mission. God calls and invites us to grow the mission.

THE MOMENTUM OF WORSHIP

As you select the three components to help strengthen your services of worship, look to the next several years. Don't try to do everything this year. Give yourself at least three years; in some instances, you may want to give yourself four or five years.

Were you to allow three years to implement your long-range plan for worship, you might focus on one of the three components in each of the years. In some instances, a component may need more than one year.

As an example, let's say we will focus on a warm and winsome spirit, dynamic and inspiring music, and power and movement in the service. We could give ourselves a

Figure 1.1

	Year 1	Year 2	Year 3
warm and winsome, welcoming and hospitable	————		
music—dynamic and inspiring	————————————		
the power and movement of the service			————

time line of one year to put a warm and winsome spirit well in place and thus would focus on that in the first year.

We might also decide to give ourselves two years to cultivate music that is more dynamic and inspiring. We would thus focus on that during years one and two, saving for year three the focus on power and movement in the service. As we can see in figure 1.1, this would be an excellent three-year plan.

Look for the rhythm and the momentum that will advance your services of worship and the timeliness that will best strengthen them. Invest the coming three years well in growing your worship services.

2:

A Hospitable Welcome

FIRST-TIME WORSHIPERS

The first major component of corporate, dynamic worship is a service that is warm and winsome, welcoming and hospitable, gracious and encouraging. Consider this question: How is your service of worship perceived by first-time worshipers? Look at the worship service through their eyes and then ask yourself,

- Is our worship service friendly and welcoming?
- Does it share a warm hospitality?
- Does the service share a welcome that is open and gracious, encouraging and helpful?

Across the years I have frequently asked congregations what one thing they like best about their church. Again and again the answer is, "We are a friendly group of people." Note: Virtually all congregations *are* friendly groups of people.

By definition the only people who are not at church are the people who did not find us friendly. They are somewhere else. In thirty-six years as a consultant, I have never had a

single person say that one of the things they liked best about
the congregation was that it was the unfriendliest group of
people they had ever had the chance to participate in.

Try to see your service of worship through the eyes of a
first-time worshiper, and then consider what they see.

Congregations can help the service of worship be warm
and winsome, welcoming and encouraging, with

- new-person greeters
- relational ushers
- pew greeters

While you could certainly do all three of these, the art is
to select the one you can do best. You might make it a point
to do the others on Christmas and Easter and other major
community Sundays. Year round, focus primarily on one of
these to help your service become more warm and welcoming in helpful ways.

New-Person Greeters

Distinct from door greeters who stand at an entrance and
welcome each person, new-person greeters stand away from
the door. They pretty well recognize those who come regularly and can therefore pick out someone who is new. They
watch for the person who appears puzzled, somewhat un-
certain as to where to go (often the signs of a first-time
worshiper).

The new-person greeter moves to the new person and
welcomes them in a warm, engaging way and usually shares
in a brief conversation. The new-person greeter's purpose is
to share hospitality. They do not hassle nor hustle the first-
time worshiper, nor do they give a great deal of church pro-
gramming information.

The tone of this first, brief visit between the new-person
greeter and the first-time worshiper is personal and rela-

tional, not institutional and organizational. It is not information seeking or information giving. The focus is a simple welcome. Over the years, another question I have asked in interviews is, Why did you decide to make this particular congregation your church home? Over and over the response has been, "The first Sunday we came, Mary so warmly welcomed us, we just knew we had found our church home." The names vary; the spirit remains the same. Consistently they were welcomed by a person who made them feel at home.

You never get a second chance to make that first impression. Often the first impression is formed during this brief visit with a new-person greeter in the few minutes before the service. It does not take large groups of persons—that can be overwhelming and intimidating. It takes just one person to make a first-time worshiper feel at home.

Eighty percent of people's decisions in choosing a new church home depends on what does or does not happen on Sunday morning. Don't trust studies that say people visit many times before they make up their minds about a church. Those studies were done only among the people who came back. None of those studies included the people who did not come back, who only visited that one time.

Imagine that you and I are going to try a new restaurant. We have never been there before—it is our first visit. Eighty percent of the decision as to whether we ever go back will be made even before we have finished our meal. It is the same with a first-time worshiper. And often the first impression people form is made by the new-person greeter's welcoming them and helping them to feel at home.

Relational Ushers

The second impression people usually have is when they sit down and look around and discover whether or not anyone around them is friendly. Some congregations have relational ushers—person-centered ushers—who help seat first-time worshipers near someone who will help them feel at home.

Ushers do not need to seat many of us, since those who attend regularly will most likely sit where they usually do and don't require any help finding that "personal pew." (In fact, some of us sometimes act like we have deeds at the county courthouse on particular pews. Churchgoers can become very attached to them!)

Many ushers are good at welcoming persons and sharing the bulletin and news sheet with them. Not all your ushers need to seat new persons. There may not be that many newcomers every Sunday. Select one to three of your ushers and encourage them to seat new people beside someone who will help them feel at home.

One congregation may have only two young couples. Everybody else in the congregation has gray hair. A relational usher will seat a first-time young couple near one of the two young couples. When the visitors look around, their second impression will be of people "like them" who are friendly and help them feel welcome.

In congregations where there may be no younger couples, the helpful relational usher will seat a first-time young couple among the best grandmothers and grandfathers in the church. Young couples do not look only for other young couples; they look for an extended family. That best grandmother or grandfather will help them to feel at home.

Pew Greeters

Another way you can achieve the same warm and welcoming second impression is with pew greeters. You don't need greeters for every pew in your church. It is highly predictable where first-time worshipers will probably sit.

Most first-time worshipers come near the time the service starts, and the available seating is often at the front of the worship auditorium or at the rear. Simply have greeters for those pews where first-time worshipers will probably be seated. The pew greeter looks forward to welcoming new persons in the three or four pews they are responsible for. This happens before and after the service.

Some churches seek to do all three—they have new-person greeters, relational ushers, and pew greeters. If you can, fine. But you don't have to do all three. The art is to select the one you can do best, and do that one well. You might decide to focus your best efforts on Christmas and Easter and your eight other major community Sundays. You might decide to focus on the fifteen or twenty Sundays a year when it is highly probable that you will have first-time worshipers. You might decide to focus on the whole year. Do one of these three well, and people will sense that your congregation is warm and winsome, welcoming and encouraging.

THE DISCOVERY OF NEW PERSONS

Whether you use new-person greeters, relational ushers, or pew greeters, select men and women who have a genuine interest in discovering new persons.

Don't choose individuals who will take this on as a responsibility and duty. They will communicate to first-time worshipers that this is a church of responsibilities and duties.

Don't select persons who are worried about the future of the church and whether it will have enough members to sustain itself. They will communicate that this is a church that worries a lot about the future and has a preoccupation with getting new members.

Choose those who enjoy people, who like to discover new persons, who are open and inviting, encouraging, helpful, and warm. You are not looking for the backslapper or the quick-talker. You are looking for people with a quiet sense of warmth, a deep spirit of joy, and a hopeful, encouraging confidence.

They will communicate that we are the Easter people, that we are the Christmas people, that we are the mission people. They will teach first-time worshipers that we are the people with confidence and assurance, grace and encouragement—here to help them with their life and destiny in the name of Christ.

You may have a regular team who shares this important welcoming work from Sunday to Sunday. You may have another team who will join to help on major community Sundays.

If you were to select new-person greeters as the one area of three on which to focus, you might proceed in this way: Have three new-person greeters regularly at your service of worship, and, on your major community Sundays, when there is a probability of having more first-time worshipers, add another three, so you will have six available greeters welcoming new persons.

Despite your efforts to organize greeters, you may miss a few first-time worshipers. Don't let this worry you. Focus more on the warmth and the welcome to be shared with first-time worshipers than on creating a foolproof, no-one-slips-through-the-cracks system. Those systems sometimes become perfectionistic and legalistic. When you focus on the ones you will welcome in a genuinely helpful and gracious spirit, you will do well.

3 :

Leadership

People develop their first impression when they come through the door. Their second impression comes as they sit down and look around. They form their third impression as they look forward toward the chancel. Does what they see there reach out warmly to them or appear remote and removed from them? Is there anyone friendly there? Our first-time worshipers gain their third impression from the leadership in the service:

- choirs
- worship leaders
- pastors

Choirs

As people sit down and look forward, one of the best things that can greet their eyes is a choir of people who have about them a warm, welcoming, and friendly spirit.

Indeed, in many congregations it would be helpful if some of the choir members would almost accidentally stumble into a smile! Too often people look at the choir and see the twins Doom and Gloom slumped shoulder to shoulder. We can almost see the cobwebs growing between them. Over the door of some churches I keep expecting to see the words clearly written, "Behold, all ye who enter here shall never smile again."

I was once in a congregation and watched the choir lead the congregation in the singing of the hymn "Joy to the World." Looking at the faces of the choir, you might have thought there had been a death in their midst. For that matter, I have been to some funeral services that have expressed a better sense of joy, confidence, and hope than some choirs on Sunday morning. It is as though they think Sunday morning is Sunday mourning.

Encourage members of the choir to have about them a warm spirit of welcome, encouragement, and invitation—to embody the spirit of Christmas, the spirit of Easter. Remember, too, that this spirit of welcome and encouragement communicates itself both in the kind of music the choir sings and in the sense of family that the choir shares with one another. This spirit will radiate out into the congregation.

Worship Leaders

Another way to help the service communicate this welcoming spirit is to have worship leaders who are warm and winsome, friendly and encouraging. Worship leaders assist the pastor in leading the worship service. A worship leader may share the announcements and lead a responsive reading. A worship leader may even lead the whole service, allowing the pastor to focus his or her best competencies on the pastoral prayer, the sermon, and the benediction. They also assist in communicating a warm welcome to all who have come together for worship.

Select as worship leaders persons who

- are warm and welcoming
- have excellent speaking ability
- have a sense of presence
- exhibit a spirit of compassion
- have character, self-esteem, integrity
- possess a spirit that matches the mission

You will notice that first on the list is the spirit of gracious hospitality—you want worship leaders who are warm and engaging and who can convey a sense of encouragement and welcome.

Be certain they have excellent speaking ability. Someone who lacks this skill can be encouraged to cultivate it, but the service of worship is not the time to practice. We are looking for worship leaders who have a solid ability to speak in public.

Select worship leaders with a sense of presence. Everyone is nervous and anxious to some extent. At the same time, the best worship leaders have a sense of calm presence and assurance about them.

Look for worship leaders who share a spirit of compassion and community. In their day-to-day life they may sometimes focus on challenge and commitment. What is important in the service of worship is their sense of compassion and their spirit of community.

It is important that worship leaders be people of character and integrity and that they possess solid self-esteem. This does not mean you are looking for "perfect" persons. We have all sinned and fallen short of the glory of God. We are looking for those who, with God's forgiveness and grace, have advanced their strength of character. They don't suffer from low self-esteem, they don't look down on themselves or think poorly of themselves. They have a healthy sense of self-worth. Their personal integrity conveys a sense of wholeness about their life.

Select worship leaders whose spirit matches the mission. If your congregation's mission is with families who have small children, your worship leaders don't have to be persons with small children. You could select persons who are among the best grandmothers and grandfathers in the church. Select your worship leaders from among those who are in tune with, in sympathy and support with, the mission.

Sometimes I'm asked how often worship leaders should be part of the services. I certainly would have worship leaders on Easter and Christmas, on major community Sundays, and on the other Sundays when you are most likely to have first-time worshipers. You don't automatically need worship leaders every Sunday. It would not be helpful to try to have worship leaders on more Sundays than you have competent persons to fill the post. Having effective worship leaders is not a matter of allowing everyone who wants a turn to have one.

In the biblical understanding, there is a diversity of gifts. Some people have gifts, strengths, and competencies that equip them to serve as worship leaders. Some people have the gifts, strengths, and competencies needed to do other things. It is important that your worship leaders be persons who do the leading well. We're not looking for people who are willing. We're looking for people who do it well.

And it is not simply a matter of rotating from one Sunday to the next. One worship leader may serve during Advent. Another person may serve as worship leader during Lent. It is helpful to have some continuity of worship leaders from Sunday to Sunday. The important point is to select people who will lead worship well.

A team understanding of leadership also appropriately includes a team understanding of worship. The pastor who

espouses a team, congregational understanding of leadership who nevertheless is always the solo person leading
worship completely contradicts that understanding. A pastor does not need to lead the whole service by himself or
herself. A pastor can share the leadership, as a team, with a
worship leader.

In many congregations with whom I work, the pastor is
a good shepherd, a helpful preacher, a wise, caring leader—
and he or she is also quiet and shy. God blesses quiet, shy
persons. And yet a quiet, shy person leading the whole worship service alone may exhaust all the "air time" available to
a quiet, shy person too soon. By the time he or she stands to
preach the sermon, the "air time" available to a quiet, shy
person is gone, and that person's own confidence and energies are used up.

A competent worship leader can significantly help a
quiet, shy pastor by freeing the pastor to focus his or her
best energies on the pastoral prayer, the sermon, and the
benediction. In that context, when the pastor stands to
preach the sermon, he or she is standing with full confidence and energy. The pastor continues the momentum the
worship leader has been building in the service.

In any number of congregations where pastors have begun to share the leadership of the service with a worship
leader, when I return for follow-up consultation a year or so
later, I find people saying how warm and encouraging their
pastor has become. In fact, their pastor continues to be a
quiet, shy person. But now, surrounded by worship leaders
who share a sense of warmth and welcome, the pastor is
perceived as warmer and more welcoming.

Pastors who want to communicate that they are good
shepherds encourage the worship leader to share whatever
announcements are made in conjunction with the service of
worship. A pastor who frequently does the announcements
teaches the congregation that he or she is a manager, a

program director, an administrator more than a shepherd and a leader.

Most important, one of the ways in which first-time worshipers can experience the warmth and welcoming spirit of a congregation is through the leadership of gifted, competent worship leaders.

Pastor

Sometimes the warm, winsome spirit of the service comes from the choir; sometimes it comes through from the worship leaders; and sometimes the best way to grow forward this spirit is through the pastor.

Warm, winsome pastors communicate a sense of confidence and assurance, grace and encouragement, joy and hope. We live in a mission field; ours is no longer a churched culture. In a mission field, I encourage pastors to pray well, think well, focus well on the following:

• Relax and be at peace.

• Have fun and enjoy life.

• Live in Christ.

It does no good for a pastor to be tense and tight, nervous and anxious. The ballplayer who goes to the plate tense and tight, determined to hit a home run on every pitch, does one thing very well—strikes out. Yes, it *is* a tough mission field, and yes, your tension and anxiety will not make it easier. What will help is to be at peace and to relax.

Jesus is clear in the New Testament: The kingdom is like a wedding feast; the kingdom is like a great banquet. The kingdom is not like a dull, dreary meeting; the kingdom is not like a solemn, serious ceremony. Have fun, enjoy life, live as a person of hope. Live as a Christmas person. Live as an Easter person. Live in joy the life God gives you.

Pastors who live in Christ share a sense of warmth and welcome. Their lives are not totally consumed by programs and activities, committee meetings and appointments, even though they will be about some of those many busy things. They primarily live in the mission. They primarily live in Christ. They see themselves as leaders in the mission to which Christ guides them.

Which of these—choir, worship leaders, or pastors—will best help improve the leadership of your worship services? Which offer the best promise of developing a spirit of warmth and winsomeness, welcome and encouragement?

THE SPIRIT OF WELCOME

In your announcements on Sunday morning, look for ways to share a spirit of welcome. And find a better greeting than this:

> "Those of you who are visiting with us this morning, we want you to know how glad we are to have you visiting with us, and we hope you will come back and visit with us again when you can."

On the surface this initially sounds well meaning. But there are three problems. First, notice how many times "you" and "us" is repeated. Every time someone says "you" and "us" a barrier is raised. It communicates that "you" are not part of "us." First-time worshipers come hoping there won't be too many barriers.

Second, the statement suggests they are "visiting." They are not simply visiting—they came to worship. Something is happening in their life. They came looking for help, hope, and home. Referring to their coming as a "visit" indicates that we are trivializing their situation.

Third, when we say, "We hope you will come back and visit with us again when you can," we confirm that we do not understand that something is happening in their life. It teaches them that we think this is simply a functional, institutional exercise in shopping around for a church home.

Instead, consider this possible greeting. You could say:

> "Those of you who are worshiping here for the first time, welcome. We are glad we can worship God together this morning. As we can be helpful, we look forward to doing so."

The spirit of this statement communicates a mutual sense of caring. There are no "you" and "us" barriers—we are worshiping together. The first-time worshiper is part of the family, is "in" from the first Sunday.

The phrase "as we can be helpful" is more shepherding than "if we can be helpful," which sounds conditional. The phrase "we look forward to doing so" is more relational and intentional, whereas the phrase "feel free to contact us" sounds more functional and organizational. With first-time worshipers, the spirit with which you share the welcoming announcement is decisive.

Let whatever registration procedure you use also share a spirit of welcome. Some congregations have newcomer cards to be filled out and placed in the offering. Some pass registration pads down the pews. Some invite persons to turn and greet those around them. And some congregations have a registry for visitors in the vestibule or narthex.

The procedure is important. The spirit with which you invite people to share in that procedure is even more important. I have been in some congregations where, in a perfunctory, routine way, people have been invited to pass registration pads down the pews. What has happened then? People have complied in a perfunctory, routine way.

I am not suggesting that one way of registration is better than another. All of these ways work well in some congregations and less well in others. What *is* consistently the case is that the spirit with which the registration invitation is shared is decisive.

When schedule and facilities permit, some congregations have a hospitality center for juice and coffee where they seek to share a warm welcome with first-time worshipers. Were you to have a hospitality center, the important thing is the relational persons and their warm, welcoming spirit.

People are not primarily looking for brochures and pamphlets, information and resources. People are really looking for a spirit of compassion and a sense of community. It is the *persons* who communicate that spirit in the hospitality center who are decisive.

WAYS FORWARD

We have discussed three ways in which your congregation can help communicate the spirit of warmth and winsomeness, especially with first-time worshipers: new-person greeters, relational ushers, pew greeters. I encourage you to select the one of these three that will be most helpful.

We have discussed three ways in which the leadership of the worship service can convey warmth and welcome in the service: choir, worship leaders, pastor. Select the one of these three that will be most helpful.

The three possibilities related to the congregation presented in chapter 2 and the three possibilities related to the leadership featured in this chapter are designed to help you find ways to improve your services of worship. Pick two possibilities as objectives—one related to the congregation and one related to the leadership—to enhance the warmth and encouragement of your worship services.

When your congregation has more than one worship service, your objectives may vary from one service to another.

You may decide that in your first worship service you will focus on new-person greeters. In your second worship service you may feel that the best way forward is with pew greeters.

In your first service of worship you may decide that the best way forward for leadership is to grow the choir's sense of warmth and winsomeness. You may decide that the best way forward in your second service is with worship leaders. The point I am making is that you do not have to use the same ways in each worship service. Tailor your choices to each service.

To enhance the warmth and the hospitality, find one way with the congregation and one way with the leadership for each worship service. That will help your first-time worshipers discover that this is a congregation of people who are welcoming and gracious in the name of Christ. Some of your regular worshipers and occasional worshipers will also experience the warmth and welcome. This will be an added plus.

PART TWO:

Dynamic and Inspiring Music

4:

A Choir's Development

The second major component of vital worship is inspiring, dynamic music, and choirs play a central role here. A well-developed choir is in tune with the mission—an instrument of grace, praise, and power. A choir develops through the creative, team efforts of both the choir members and the choir director.

A choir, as I use the term, is a music grouping with strength and size. It is more than an ensemble. Choirs do not always wear robes; choirs do not always sit in the chancel. The mark of a well-developed choir is the music it shares in tune with the mission, not whether it wears robes or sits up front.

While most choirs are only vocal groupings, some choirs include a mix of both vocal and instrumental capabilities. In these choirs the persons with vocal abilities and the persons with instrumental abilities are so closely interwoven they form one cohesive unit. Such a choir is more than a vocal group occasionally accompanied by an instrumental group. It is a unified music grouping. Thus, it is important to have an expanded understanding of what a well-developed choir is—and can be.

These ten principles will help you as you grow forward your congregation's choirs:

1. Music constitutes 40 percent of the worship service
2. Fifteen to 20 percent of those who attend on Sundays are potential recruits for the choir
3. One person singing in the choir draws one to three others to church (the 1:1–3 principle)
4. Choirs give participants a sense of family
5. The best choirs have both quality and quantity
6. Each service needs its own distinctive choir
7. Because choirs are important relational groupings, they provide key ways to involve newcomers
8. Choirs tend to grow best in multiples rather than by adding one person at a time
9. A personal invitation to attend a rehearsal—not to join the choir—is the best way to recruit new choir members
10. Choir growth is determined by rehearsal space, chancel space, music selection, and the choir director

MUSIC IS 40 PERCENT OF WORSHIP

Music contributes 40 percent of the service's power and impact, its movement and momentum. I have been known to say that when my own preaching is off, I count on the music to carry the service. I have worked with many excellent pastors, good shepherds, wise, caring leaders, whose preaching—rated on a scale of one to ten—was realistically a seven. Surrounded by music that is dynamic and inspiring, the congregation hears the preaching as a nine. When the music isn't contributing its usual share, the pastor's preaching is perceived as only a five.

In one congregation I worked with, a number of people confided in me that their pastor's preaching "isn't what it used to be." As I reflected on that, I remembered a comment someone had made during an interview—"Betty is doing the best she can." That was the clue.

As I explored further, I learned that Mary had been the choir director for a number of years and had done an excellent job. She had developed a choir of thirty-five persons, who had delivered 40 percent of the service in extraordinary ways. Then Mary was transferred in her work to another part of the country.

Betty was a pretty, young, homegrown girl who had been asked to fill the vacant position. In her time as choir director, Betty had successfully grown the choir downward to fourteen persons. Choir directors grow choirs forward or downward to the number of people they can say grace over. She could say grace over only fourteen persons. And a choir of fourteen struggles to deliver 40 percent of the service of worship, particularly when for years there had been a choir of thirty-five.

People felt that the service did not have the same dynamic it once had, but they thought surely it could not be the fault of this pretty, homegrown young woman "doing the best she can" as choir director. It must have something to do with their pastor's preaching.

As the result of the consultation, we put in place a process that would help Betty enhance her skills as choir director. The choir eventually grew from fourteen to nearly thirty again. The music became more dynamic. And of course people began to say, "Our pastor's preaching has really gotten better." It is a matter of perception. The change was really in the music rather than in the preaching. Music is the soul and spirit of the service of worship.

AIMING FOR A CHOIR THAT IS
15 TO 20 PERCENT OF THE CONGREGATION

Fifteen to 20 percent of average worship attendance is recruitable as a choir. In congregations with an average worship attendance of one hundred, a potential choir of fifteen to twenty is there. Sometimes they are all already together as a choir, sitting at the front. Some may still be sitting in the congregation, not yet having discovered their place of leadership in the choir.

A congregation with an average worship attendance of three hundred has a potential choir of fifty. Although we sometimes find a choir of fifteen to twenty in that situation, it could be a choir of forty-five to sixty.

The old theory said that 10 percent of average worship attendance was recruitable as a choir. That 10 percent figure included these limiting factors:

- The notion was that everyone who sang in the choir (or nearly everyone) should be able to read music and sing on pitch immediately.

- The notion was that the choir would sing only "quality music."

- The notion was that very little time would be allotted to recruiting and coaching new choir members.

An average worship attendance of 100 really represents more people than that. Some people come once a month; some come three times a year; some come every Sunday. And so a congregation that averages 100 in worship attendance is really a pool of 150–175 persons. It takes more than 100 people to create an average worship attendance of 100.

Regrettably, in a churched culture, recruiting for the choir was done primarily among only those people who came to church every Sunday. In our time, choirs are part of the mission of the congregation, and the choir does its recruiting with

- the people who come regularly every Sunday
- the pool of people who come now and then
- the people in the community who are not yet participating in church

A mission understanding of choir recruiting searches in all of these areas. A churched-culture understanding of choir recruiting searches only among those who attend regularly. When you have a mission understanding, 15 to 20 percent of an average worship attendance is recruitable as a choir. As a matter of fact, participating in the choir is one of the major ways in which people learn their Christian faith, as well as share it.

THE 1:1–3 PRINCIPLE

The 1:1–3 principle simply stated means that one person who sings in the choir draws one to three people to worship. We see this especially when a children's choir sings. It is also true with adult choirs. It is true as well with instrumentalists, bands, orchestras, and handbells. One person who participates in some music group in a service of worship will draw one to three people to worship.

Some of the one to three people are family; some are friends; some are acquaintances. Some are persons in the congregation who are drawn more regularly to participating in worship because of the strength of the music. Some are persons in the community who are drawn to a service of worship that has the power of stirring and inspiring music. The more persons who participate in the music program, the more persons who are drawn to participate in worship.

A FAMILY SPIRIT

A choir is ultimately a relational grouping; it is very much a family. It is often among the most significant relational groupings in a congregation. Many people pursue their life's pilgrimage through the roots, the place and belonging, and the sharing and caring of the choir family.

Again and again in interviews across the years, I have learned that most people who participate in adult choirs perceive them as their family. It may also be a group for music and worship leadership. These have become among the most significant relational groupings in their life. When they go to rehearsal, it is like going to a family gathering. When they sing in the service of worship, they sing together as family.

THE NEED FOR BOTH QUALITY AND QUANTITY

Congregations that have music that is dynamic and inspiring have choirs that feature both strength and numbers. When they sing, you hear strength in the music; when they sing, you're aware of a healthy number of voices. The old notion "We prefer quality, not quantity" is precisely that— an old and foolish notion. When someone uses that phrase, they are teaching me that

- they don't have the necessary competencies to do recruiting and coaching;
- they're too busy with other things to do the recruiting and coaching; or
- they have a narrow, elitist understanding of the choir as solely a performance group.

I see many choirs that include both quality and quantity. There is no need to say, "We prefer quality to quantity."

You can have both. Yes, it may take several years of recruiting and coaching to help people advance their voices so that you have both the strength and the size, the quality and the quantity.

I take issue with the notion that growing quantity thereby sacrifices quality. It is the task of the choir director and the leaders of the various choir sections to coach people so they learn how to sing on key and so the music is well done. You can coach persons to sing. People want to learn to sing.

Helping people discover how to sing is giving them a great gift that will enrich their life. They can take their singing with them everywhere they go. Having the confidence and ability to sing helps them enrich the ordinary times of their life. Their singing helps them to rejoice in times of celebration and to endure the tough times. Singing is a rare, precious gift. Focus both on strength and size, and you will do well.

A CHOIR FOR EACH SERVICE

Develop a distinctive choir for each service. When you decide to launch a new service of worship, develop a specific choir for it.

Some churches don't do this. Instead, oddly and regrettably, they ask the present choir, which is doing well with the one service of worship, also to "cover" the new service of worship. Choir members are invited, sometimes pressed, to sing at both services, and this depletes the energy and focus of the existing choir. It scares away many potential new choir members. It ignores the opportunity to grow a new, significant relational grouping.

We will discuss this more fully in chapter 11, which focuses on developing and growing a new service of worship.

For the moment, it is important to note that for each service of worship it is best to have a choir dedicated to that particular service.

I've attended services of worship where there is no choir. Usually it is the first service on Sunday morning. There may be an occasional soloist or instrumentalist, but no choir. People make excuses for the missing music by saying, "Well, we started this service to relieve the crowded conditions at eleven o'clock" or "We started this service to reach a group of people we were not reaching at eleven o'-clock, and since we couldn't get the choir to sing at this service, we do a sort of shortened version."

By saying this they are acknowledging that a void exists; they know that 40 percent of the service is not there. But they are asking us to not pay attention to the void. The first service becomes just the "warm-up" service for the "real" service, which happens at eleven o'clock. This is the practice service.

An important opportunity is lost. In most places on the planet, you can grow a worship attendance at a first service that is virtually equal to that of a second service *when you have a full service.*

The first worship service is, in fact, the only service the people who come to that service will participate in that week. It is not as though they stay around to hear how good the choir sounds át eleven o'clock before they go home.

And it is not just the choir's anthem that is noticeably missing. The choir's strong voices help the congregation with the singing of the hymns. They bring strength and momentum to the singing of the choral responses. They provide a large part of the service's movement and inspiration.

When the choir is missing, we miss out on more than just the anthem. It's like ordering a meal at a restaurant and not getting 40 percent of it. We probably wouldn't go to that restaurant again.

When you have a choir for each service, each choir's energy is focused on its specific service. It sings at only one service, which increases the likelihood of recruiting new choir members. Because each choir is its own significant relational grouping, the more choirs you have, the more opportunities you provide for people to find roots, place, and belonging in church.

Be sure to have a choir for each service. Your worship, your congregation, and your mission will benefit.

CHOIRS OFFER NEWCOMERS A PLACE OF BELONGING

As you grow a choir, you are growing a grouping. Some people find their sense of belonging in an adult Sunday school class, and some people find their place in a women's or men's organization. Some people find their primary grouping in the choir.

The more choirs you have, the more significant rela tional groupings you offer people in your church. The fewer choirs you have, the more you limit the possibilities available to people when they seek a grouping that suits them and is helpful to them.

In our time, people generally have their first contact with a church as that church reaches out to them in mission or visitation. Their next contact is usually through participation in a service of worship. Then, having decided that this church can be home, they begin to look around for a significant relational grouping to which they can belong and in which they can find a sense of roots, family, and friendship.

If they don't find that grouping within six to eighteen months after they began to worship with us, they will join that large group called "inactives," and we will scarcely see them again. I can't overemphasize how important it is for congregations to start new groupings—and starting a new choir is an excellent opportunity for this.

The basic principle is that new people join new groupings. A new grouping is one that has been in existence less than five years. An old grouping is one that has been in existence for more than five years. It has nothing to do with gray hair and age; it has to do with the fact that the group has been together a long time. This applies to adult Sunday school classes as well as to adult choirs.

When you organize a new service of worship, you can use this opportunity to start a new grouping for persons who plan to be part of the new service. By asking the present choir to sing in the new service, you close off an opportunity you have been given.

One advantage of starting a new adult choir for that new service is that you don't have to find a new Sunday school classroom for them. They will use the rehearsal space used by the present choir, rehearsing at a separate time and developing their own sense of cohesiveness.

The more new groupings you start, the more new people you will reach. This principle applies both to Sunday school classes and adult choirs. Most congregations are wise enough to have more than one adult Sunday school class or adult study group. We can have an adult choir for each service of worship.

CHOIRS GROW IN MULTIPLES

Choirs grow in threes to fives, eights to twenties. That is my shorthand way of saying that choirs often grow by three persons at a time rather than one person at a time.

New people find new people. For example, in a choir that has been together for a long time, three new persons come to a rehearsal on a Wednesday evening. These three new people will find one another and get acquainted. The presence of the other new persons helps each become a part of the choir.

Yes, they discover a feeling of family among the old-time members of the choir. And, most important, they begin to share a sense of family with the two other new persons they have found that evening. They begin to feel that they belong with the whole choir more quickly.

By contrast, here is how it often works when one new person goes to a choir rehearsal. The choir is warm, welcoming, and encouraging. And yet that single new person's probability of continuing with this choir is very low.

The new person discovers that she is the lone visitor that evening. Before and after the rehearsal, she finds that people do come up and speak to her, welcome her, and tell her to please come back again. Yet those same people then move on to visit with the friends they've known for years, and it isn't an inclusive conversation. The new person still feels like an outsider.

Focus your invitations to new persons toward specific rehearsals, so that you help several new people to show up for the same rehearsal. They will find one another, and the shared sense of newness will help them over the hump. Choirs often grow several persons at a time, not one by one.

This same principle applies to beginning a new choir. If you decide to begin a new choir for a new worship service, things will go better the more people you have present for the first rehearsal. Fifteen will be more comfortable than five or six showing up for that first rehearsal. When only five or six people make up a choir, they begin to feel that they're practically singing solos during the Sunday morning worship service. Although it may be hard to find fifteen people, it is easier to start with fifteen and grow to twenty and twenty-five than it is to start with five or six and grow that venture forward.

A choir already in existence will grow several persons at a time. People have confidence in themselves and in the choir when they see they're not the only new person in the choir. With a new choir, as best you can, begin with fifteen and grow quickly to twenty and more.

INVITE NEW SINGERS TO A REHEARSAL, NOT TO JOIN UP

The best way to help new people become part of your choir is to invite them to a rehearsal. Don't ask them to join the choir—that's like asking someone to get married before you've even had the first date. Invite them to a rehearsal. Were you to invite ten persons to a rehearsal, four would come and three would join. Were you to invite the same ten persons to join the choir, most of them would respond, "Well, I would like to consider that some day, but right now I don't think I can."

When you invite people to a rehearsal, it's as if you were inviting them on a first date. Their commitment starts gradually, even tentatively, just as in human relationships. A couple goes out on the first date; then they date again, and again; they go steady and become engaged; then they decide to get married. The best way to grow the choir is to start with the simple invitation to a rehearsal.

When is a choir at its best? At the rehearsal! It is during rehearsals that choirs have good fun, good times, laughing, joking, and sharing with one another. During rehearsals people share their sense of being family with one another. It's the time when people hug and hold one another in life's tough, tight times, helping and shepherding, richly sharing with one another.

Certainly during the rehearsal the choir also works hard to master the music that will help persons experience the grace of God in their life. Still, by inviting people to a rehearsal, you're inviting them to experience the choir when it's at its best as family.

GUIDELINES FOR GROWTH

When I find a choir that is growing, both in strength and size, I know I have found a choir (1) that has adequate rehearsal space; (2) that has room to expand in the chancel; (3) that sings music they like to sing; and (4) that has a director who is growing his or her own competencies as a choir director.

Sometimes in working with congregations, I find a choir that has not grown in strength or size for a number of years. The first thing I do is look at the rehearsal space. Choirs never grow any larger than the space in which they rehearse. I can walk into the empty choir room, count the number of chairs, and know the outer limit of the size of that choir. Sometimes the solution to helping the choir grow, therefore, is to discover a larger rehearsal space.

The second thing I look at is the chancel space. Choirs never grow any larger than the size and space available to them in the chancel. Regrettably, there was a time in church architecture when music was thought of as an incidental, negligible part of the service. Then came a time in church architecture when music was thought of as being "performed" by small, high-quality groups. During both of those periods in church architecture, the amount of space allotted for the choir in the chancel was minimal.

One creative solution to the problem of limited chancel space is enlarging the chancel. Another solution is choosing to be a "family choir," where choir members sit in the congregation with their families. This solution also overcomes one objection to singing in the choir—namely, many people prefer to worship while sitting with their families. Fine. The choir members sit with their families in the congregation. There are extraordinary advantages to this:

- The choir is in a stronger position to help the congregation sing the hymns and choral responses.

- The choir feels more a part of the congregation in the worship service and less like a performance group.

- It is easy for the choir to come forward to share their anthem.

- More people are interested in joining this type of family choir than in joining a small performance choir that separates itself from the rest of the congregation.

Whenever a choir is not growing in strength and size, I also look at the spirit and kind of music the choir is singing. People are drawn to choirs that sing music they like to sing.

It's a strange thing. I don't know why people are this way. People have a tendency not to join a choir that sings music they don't like. By the same token, people have a strong tendency to join choirs that sing the kind of music they love.

A choir that is not growing will sometimes give the age-old excuse "We are singing quality music." They sing music they think "should" be sung. And yet the spirit and style of their music do not persuade people to want to invest their time in rehearsing and singing. Sometimes the key to growing a strong choir is to expand the variety of its music. You'll thereby increase the likelihood of drawing new choir members, because they know they'll get a chance to sing music they like to sing.

The fourth factor I look at when the choir is not growing in strength and size is the competency of the choir director. When the choir director stops growing, the choir stops growing. When the choir director is growing, the choir is growing.

Sometimes when a choir director has quit growing in competency, when she has grown as far as she can or will for that moment in time, the church has two options for improvement. You can help the choir director discover ways to develop her skills, or you can search for a new director who can better cultivate the strength and size of your choir.

A choir director almost unconsciously grows a choir forward or downward to a membership that matches the director's competencies. I've seen a choir director take a struggling choir with ten to twelve persons and build it into an extraordinary choirs of forty-plus persons. And even though a director may inherit a thirty-five member choir, it is possible that he will dwindle that choir to fourteen if that is the size choir that matches his competencies. When you see the strength and size of the choir, you are seeing the competencies of the choir director; there is a direct correlation.

When you consider the factors affecting your choir's growth, look at the rehearsal space, the chancel space, the spirit and kind of music, and the competencies of the choir director.

I have a deep appreciation for what choirs bring to a service of worship. The ten principles discussed in this chapter will be helpful to you as you grow forward the choirs in your congregation.

At stake is more than an anthem on Sunday morning. The music is the soul and spirit of the service. It is through the music that people's hearts are touched, their souls are stirred, their hopes are lifted. The choir helps the congregation sing the hymns and the choral responses. The choir contributes in vital ways to the service's momentum and spirit.

5:

The Vital Role of Excellent Choir Directors

A CHOIR DIRECTOR'S COMPETENCIES

I hope it is evident that I have a deep, abiding appreciation for what excellent choirs and choir directors contribute to the worship service. Wherever I find dynamic and inspiring worship services, I find excellent choir directors. When I find congregations in trouble with their service of worship, many times there is a mismatch between the competencies of the person who is choir director and the competencies needed for the task.

The following list of competencies can help the choir director to develop his or her competencies. Many choir directors who are enhancing their skills have established a consulting team to help them. You will discover specific resources for coaching and consulting teams in my book *Effective Church Leadership*.

Many choir directors (both staff and volunteer) focus on the following areas as they strive to strengthen their skills. The list may also be useful to your congregation as an evaluation tool when searching for a new choir director; it can serve as a guide to determining which competencies each candidate brings to the task.

Recruiting

Back in the days of a churched culture, when going to church was "the thing to do," choir directors could ignore—or give less attention to—recruiting new members. Now, when going to church is no longer a given, and churches have to view their culture as a mission field, a director's ability to recruit people to be part of the choir is a significant skill.

As you interview candidates for your position of choir director, or as you search for a competent volunteer, evaluate who among the possible candidates has significantly grown a choir in recent years. It is a demonstrably quantifiable competency. If a director started with a choir of ten or twelve and expanded it to thirty-five or forty over three or four years, that candidate has a strong recruiting competency.

Coaching

When a choir director says with quiet assurance, "I am confident I can help any person who can talk learn to sing," he is teaching you that he has a coaching competency. Should a choir director tell you, "I will take only those who already read music," he is teaching you that he does not have a coaching competency.

Choir directors with a coaching competency invest time in giving people voice lessons. They hold teaching sessions with two or three persons from the choir. By coaching them in individual and small-group rehearsals, they help these people grow forward their abilities as participants in the choir.

A choir director with a coaching competency has the ability to take some of us who sing well in the shower on Saturday night and help us to sing well to the glory of God on Sunday morning. Lots of people sing or hum along with the radio as they drive in their car. They sing in various ways in day-to-day life. A choir director with a coaching competency gives people an extraordinary gift by helping them to sing well every day as well as on Sunday morning.

Motivating Others Through Compassion and Community

In our time, choirs respond best to and are motivated by a spirit of compassion and community. What ultimately draws and holds choir members is their sense of the director's deep compassion for them and the spirit of community they find with other members of the choir.

Some choirs will put up with the challenges posed by the director and the time commitments required, but not because they are drawn to the challenge of some difficult piece of music or because they want to impress the choir director with the depth of their commitment. They will work long and hard, not because of words of challenge and commitment, but because they have discovered the spirit of compassion and the sense of community in this choir. Look for a choir director who motivates primarily by drawing on the resources of compassion and community.

Shepherding

The choir is finally a family, and among the shepherds of that family is the choir director. The choir will have other shepherds as well—certain persons in the soprano, alto, tenor, and bass sections who take the lead in times of celebration and in times of tragedy. It is also important and helpful for the choir director to be one of the significant shepherds of the choir.

Preparation

You're looking for a person who has developed the competency to prepare in advance for the rehearsal and for the service. You're looking for a person who is searching and discovering music, new and inspiring, and who invests time with the worship leaders and the pastor in developing the service. And you're looking for a person who takes the time to learn the music well before presenting it to the choir.

The choir members experience this when they arrive at rehearsal and find the music selections laid out for them in advance; their music folders are prepared before rehearsal starts. This competency of preparation shows in the rehearsal; the choir director has learned the music in advance and knows it well. This shows respect for the choir members' time by making the best use of the time available for rehearsal.

You're not looking for a person who walks into rehearsal and says, "Well, what shall we sing this coming Sunday?" Neither are you looking for a person who repeatedly draws on a reservoir of old anthems learned twenty or thirty years ago.

Vocal Ability

You are looking for a person who has developed a choral competency. They have vocal ability rather than instrumental ability. They understand the voice.

We too often ask people who are skilled in some other area of music to be the choir director. This is unfair. Simply because a person plays the piano or the organ—even extra-ordinarily well—it does not automatically mean she can lead a choir well. When a person with an instrumental competency ends up as choir director, the choir ends up accompanying her playing of the organ. You are looking for a person who has competencies in the choral and vocal areas of music.

Leading a Group

A soloist may have an outstanding vocal music competency, but that does not mean she would make a good choir director. I sometimes see choir directors who really function as soloists. They have an individual competency. The choir ends up accompanying their solo. These vocalists don't have what it takes to lead a choral group.

To have a group competency means being able to take an array of individuals who are "sometimes sopranos, almost altos, occasionally tenors, and now and then basses" and weave them together as one rich choral voice, singing well to the glory of God. A soloist has an individual competency. A choir director has a group competency.

Fruitful Rehearsals

Someone may have a sense of presence on Sunday morning during the service of worship and, at the same time, may not yet have learned how to lead an excellent rehearsal. One of the primary factors in growing the strength and size of a choir is the director's ability to lead excellent rehearsals.

I encourage churches to have a prospective choir director lead a rehearsal; don't invite someone to be a choir director without first doing this. Whether you're looking for a volunteer, a part-time, or full-time choir director, when you have narrowed the possibilities to the final two or three candidates, give each of those candidates the opportunity to lead a choir rehearsal.

When you are hiring a typist, you want to confirm the person's competency in typing. Likewise, it is in rehearsal that you will discover whether a candidate for choir director has a competency in leading rehearsals.

Contributing to Worship

Look for a person who has a sense of presence in the service of worship and who is fully present during the entire service. You are not looking for someone who merely comes awake when the choir does the anthem. You want a choir director who both fully worships and actively participates throughout the entire service.

Look for a person who has the flexibility to help the music match the message for the morning. With a spirit of grace and teamwork, good choir directors will build the music—even during the service of worship—in ways that contribute to the power and movement of the service.

Furthermore, topics announced in the worship bulletin do not always match what is actually preached. And even with the best planning, the pastor, in the pastoral prayer and the sermon, may be led in a direction during the service that was not anticipated. It is helpful for services of worship to be open to the leading of the spirit. And it is helpful for a choir director, as the service unfolds, to have the capability to adjust and match the music with the message.

One choir director with whom I have worked is confident and competent in his role and is trusted and respected by the leadership of the church as well as by the pastoral team. As he listens to the pastoral prayer, he selects the choral response that suits it. The closing hymn is not selected in advance. As he listens to the sermon, he selects the last hymn, one that matches the message. As he listens to

the benediction, he selects the choral response appropriate
to it. He is able to pull the music selections together almost
spontaneously, and demonstrates an extraordinary competency in participating in leading the service of worship.

Working As a Team

In our time—in a mission field—it is central that we work
and share together as a team. This means that the choir director will bring strong, solid, mature leadership to the
team—with a spirit of mutual trust and respect. This is not
a time for players who hog the ball and refuse to pass to
anyone else on the team. This is not a time for empire
builders or for prima donnas who insist on their own way
all the time. Nor is it a time for complainers and whiners.

Count on a competent choir director to have a strong
sense of direction and leadership. Count on the person to
have a definite sense of confidence and purpose. You would-
n't want it any other way. It wouldn't help to settle for a
team player who was mediocre.

To be sure, a strong team will not always agree. And yet
as a team, it will find a way forward. It will be more than a
collection of separate departments.

When recruiting a choir director, look for these ten competencies. You may not find all ten fully present in a potential
choir director. Look for the person who has seven of these
competencies well in place and has a clear plan for growing
and developing his competencies.

In order to support your choir director's professional
growth, help her identify which of these ten she already has
well in place, which she plans to develop, and which new
ones she looks forward to improving during the coming
three years.

WHERE TO SEARCH

In searching for a choir director, your search team can look in the following areas:

1. Educational Circles Look in elementary school, junior high/middle school, high school, college, and university circles. Frequently the best choir directors are found in these areas.

2. Professional Music Circles Look among the leaders of professional music groups in the area, those whose vocation is commercial music. Excellent choir directors frequently come from among people who sing or write or record music professionally.

3. Civic and Community Circles Many communities have volunteer civic groups that perform drama or music. You may find a volunteer in, or a leader of, one of these groupings who would make an excellent choir director.

4. Business Circles Some people with strong music backgrounds have, for a variety of reasons, found their way into other professions. They may be contractors, carpenters, stockbrokers, secretaries, nurses, doctors. Whatever their current profession, they may also have the training and the competencies to be excellent choir directors.

5. Not-for-Profit Circles In the American Heart Association, the Boy Scouts or Girl Scouts, and other such organizations, there are musically competent persons. Sometimes they are volunteers; sometimes they are on the staff of these groups. What you will already know about them is that they have the competency to work well in a not-for-profit environment.

6. Retired Circles Although their vocations may not have been directly related to music, many retired people have the makings of excellent choir directors. It may well be that your best candidate for choir director will be found among retired people in your community.

7. Persons Working at Home   Once their children are old enough, some people who have been working at home find themselves free to pursue their musical competencies and longings. They will be among the best choir directors your congregation has ever had.

8. Religious Circles   Look for a choir director among strong, healthy, stable and growing, or rapidly growing congregations. They will have the kind of experience that will help grow your own congregation's worship through their music and leadership.

Be cautious about a choir director who comes from a congregation that is static or declining. Although this person may be among "the best music people in the community," he may also have learned the behavior patterns that contribute to a church's deterioration.

The decline of the church he is serving is certainly not entirely his fault. At the same time, unfortunately, his experiences in a church that lacks a strong, healthy character may carry over into his new position. If you hire him, there may well be a year or two of first-blush enthusiasm; but his mind-set from being around a dying or no-growth congregation will eventually permeate your setting, and you will be disappointed in the resulting music program.

Given a choice, select a choir director from a strong, healthy, firmly established, or rapidly growing church, someone who has learned and is accustomed to these behavior patterns. That person will more likely be able to help your church stabilize and grow.

I have intentionally listed this eighth area as the last place in which to search. Many of the best choir directors with whom I've had the privilege of working across the years have come from one of the first seven areas just listed.

I would, then, recommend that you look in these seven areas. These are where many congregations find their best choir directors.

Go ahead and look in religious circles. Be aware, however, that just because someone has served as choir director in another church, it does not mean that she will automatically know how to build a dynamic music program in your church. What she may know how to do is plan music for a church that is not growing. You've already had enough help in that direction, thank you. What you want is a person who will come and strengthen the mission of your congregation by providing inspiring music.

Your team may want to search in all eight areas or in just five that appear to be the most promising in your community. You're looking for someone who is happy where he is, with what he is now accomplishing. He will come and be happy with you, with what he is achieving with your congregation. Generally, you are not looking for someone who is unhappy and wants to leave. She may come and be unhappy with you and want to leave as well.

ORGANIZING FOR AN ACTIVE SEARCH

One helpful way to discover a new choir director is to select a search team of five persons. They might do the usual things such as running an ad in appropriate church publications and studying the resultant resumes. Most important, the best thing a search team can do is actively search. The team should not look for quick closure; it should not select the first candidate it finds—unless, of course, that candidate is the best!

This team can begin by identifying five of the aforementioned areas that are the most promising sources in your community (and, sometimes, in your region of the country). Each person on the search team focuses on one of the five areas. To be sure, the whole search team keeps its eyes and ears open in all of the areas, while each has a primary responsibility to search thoroughly in one area.

Within the area for which they have responsibility, each member of the search team networks with key leaders and key groups. Each should talk with successful persons in their area and, as appropriate, circulate the word in key publications of that area. They should encourage people in the congregation and friends of the church in the community to actively search as well. This is an active search, not a passive search. It is an open, public search, not a closed, secretive search. We are looking for one of the most important persons to help us with our mission in the community—one who will help us to develop stirring, inspiring worship. Thus, we search actively and well.

Frequently, we must invest three to five months in a strong search. When looking for a new choir director for a current worship service, it is often helpful to invite someone to be an interim choir director. When looking for a choir director to develop the choir for a new service, we might begin the search at least four months prior to when the new service will begin.

Search well in the beginning and you will discover an excellent match. It will prove more rewarding to invest constructive time at the beginning of the relationship. It is much tougher and a lot less fun to find someone quickly and later discover it is not a good match and then try to figure out what to do. A strong active search is more helpful to everyone and will best advance the mission.

ENHANCING THE DIRECTOR'S GROWTH

Life is a search and a pilgrimage where opportunities for growth abound. You'll most likely find a choir director who brings seven of the ten competencies discussed earlier in this chapter. The art is to help the choir director identify

- of the seven now well in place, which two competencies he or she wants to develop, and
- of the three not well in place, which two competencies he or she plans to develop.

When you have a choir director who is intentionally furthering her current strengths and adding new strengths, you will also have a choir that is furthering its current strengths and adding new strengths. It is true that a choir contributes to the growth of a choir director. It is equally true that the growth of the choir director contributes to the growth of the choir.

As you bring a new director on board, help him to identify the capabilities he now has firmly in place that he plans to advance in the coming three years. Help him also to identify the competencies he does not yet have as well in place that he plans to develop in the coming three years.

Don't wait to have this conversation two years after the new director has arrived. When he accepts the position, help him to identify right then his areas of growth. The choir will mirror his development.

THE TIME INVESTMENT, AND PAYING FOR IT

If you could have only three persons on your church staff, I would encourage you to have a pastor, an administrative assistant who will double the effectiveness of the pastor, and a choir director.

I think it's important that the congregation be fair and reasonable in terms of the stipend offered for the time an excellent choir director invests. Take seriously the amount of time these valuable choir directors spend on their various activities as illustrated in table 5.1, which shows the approximate number of hours per week needed in doing each.

Regrettably, many churches with a choir director on the staff base the stipend merely on the two hours for the rehearsal and the two hours related to the service of worship. When a church pays for only four hours, it usually gets what it pays for.

It takes approximately fifteen hours a week, year round, to build a strong choir. The recruiting is done weekly, not once a year. Excellent choir directors visit people, phone them, write notes, work with the choir recruiting team, and invest about two hours a week in reaching persons who come regularly to worship, who come occasionally to worship, and who are in the community. Recruiting is a major task, and it takes time.

The best choir directors invest approximately three hours a week in coaching. They come early before the rehearsal to work with individuals and small groups; they take time on Saturday morning to work with persons in individual voice lessons.

The best choirs are highly motivated choirs. It is the personal note saying "Thank you," the phone call positively affirming someone, the special effort to show appreciation to the choir. It easily takes an hour a week to motivate a choir with these efforts at building people up.

Table 5.1 A Choir Director's Weekly Investment of Time

Recruiting	2 hours	Rehearsal	2 hours
Coaching	3 hours	Worship	2 hours
Motivating	1 hour	Team	1 hour
Shepherding	1 hour		
Preparation	3 hours	Total:	15 hours

Shepherding happens in good times, celebration times—birthdays, anniversaries, promotions. Shepherding is also needed in life's tough, tight times when trouble comes. It's not that the choir director will regularly invest one hour each week in shepherding. Rather, throughout the year the choir director will have averaged at least an hour a week in shepherding with the choir.

Preparation takes approximately three hours a week. The choir director who is preparing is growing. The choir director who isn't preparing is the choir director who is dying. When the choir director is dying, the choir dies. It is preparation for the music that matches the mission and the message; it's the kind of preparation that searches for the exact piece of music that will distinctively communicate the gospel within a particular worship service.

There is the rehearsal time and the time before and after the worship service as well as the service itself. Add to this the time meeting with the worship team and the pastor.

These activities average fifteen hours a week. This is more than the rehearsal and the service. Developing and improving one choir easily requires a fifteen-hours-a-week commitment. It is fair and reasonable to offer a staff person a stipend that's commensurate with the time needed to do the job well. Share in a mutual evaluation of the progress annually.

When you pay for four hours—two hours of rehearsal, two hours on Sunday morning—what you will mostly get is four hours. You'll also get a choir that at best doesn't grow and at worst dries up. When you invest in a choir director by offering a stipend that is fair for the fifteen hours, you invest in a growing director and a growing choir.

The simplest way to grow the giving in your congregation is to grow the worship attendance. Were your average attendance 100, and your total giving $100,000, if you increased the average worship attendance to around 120, the giving would grow to around $120,000. There is a direct correlation between worship attendance and giving. There is no direct correlation between membership and giving.

The simplest way to grow the worship attendance is to grow the choir. If you started with a choir of ten and an average worship attendance of 100 and built the choir to twenty, the ten new choir members would draw a new ten to thirty persons to worship. Conservatively speaking, the average worship attendance would grow to 120, and the giving would grow to $120,000.

If you are currently budgeting $2,000 for a director who leads a choir of ten, for instance, consider what would happen if you invested an additional $4,000 in a director (continue with the same person or look for a new one) who can grow the choir to twenty. You will have invested an additional $4,000, and the "net new giving" will be the $20,000, minus the $4,000, or $16,000 in new giving. A choir director who can grow the choir to twenty can grow it up to thirty, and now you're at $130,000 in total giving.

Frequently we're shortsighted. We focus only on the rehearsal and worship time. When you invest in an excellent choir director, you will have more than sufficient net new giving to cover your investment. Take seriously the value of the music, the time that it really takes a choir director to build a strong choir, and pay a fair, reasonable stipend for that total time. Establish mutual goals with the choir director for choir growth as part of the job description. Your music will become even more dynamic and inspiring.

6:

Music Possibilities

ELEVEN MUSIC RESOURCES TO DRAW ON

Although choirs and choir directors have a decisive impact, there are actually eleven possibilities for strengthening the music in your worship services. Comparatively few congregations have all of these possibilities well in place; indeed, very few congregations need to have all of them well in place. The art is to select six of the eleven and to develop these.

The major music resources that will help your services of worship to be corporate and dynamic, stirring and inspiring, and helpful and hopeful include

- Congregational singing
- Major adult choirs
- Choir directors
- Special vocal music: solos, ensembles
- Instrumentalists
- Children's choirs
- Youth choirs

- Special choirs
- Festivals and community events
- Retreats and resource leaders
- Keyboard music

Each of these possibilities will contribute a dynamic quality to worship. And with six of them well in place, you will have significant momentum in your music program, adding extraordinary power to your worship services.

When you have more than one service of worship, develop each service with its own specific set of six of these possibilities. You don't need the same six in all services. Thus you can tailor the specific six to the particular congregation you seek to reach and help with each service of worship. Further, all six don't need to be fully present each week. Simply be sure to deliver six of the eleven with strength and consistency.

Congregational Singing

One of the many strengths that effective, successful congregations have in their worship services is congregational singing—the singing of hymns, choruses, choral responses, and refrains.

People learn the Christian faith as they sing the Christian hymns. The hymnal and songbook are the primary "Bible" many persons read. People discover both the content and the spirit of the gospel as they sing the hymns of mission.

In some congregations a song leader assists with the singing. When I say "song leader," I do not mean someone who stands up front moving their arms as though directing a choir. I have more in mind a person whose strong voice and obvious joy in singing inspires the congregation's confidence and joy as they sing.

The choir accompanies the congregation, giving them confidence to "make a joyful noise" to the Lord. I've heard people say, "I love to sit next to Nancy. What comes out of her mouth when she sings is exactly what comes out of my heart." The choir helps the congregation sing from their heart. Congregational singing is decisive in helping people discover the Christian faith and live the Christian life.

Major Adult Choirs and Choir Directors

We've already discussed the value of adult choirs and choir directors. What I want to affirm is that a distinctive, major adult choir for each service advances the music for that service. Some congregations have two services of worship; some have three or four. It is best for each service to be led by its own adult choir or distinctive music group.

This will be discussed further in the chapter on developing new worship services. For the moment, let it be simply observed that it is not appropriate for one adult choir to assume it has a proprietary monopoly as the only adult choir for all worship services, any more than one adult Sunday school class would assume it should be the class for all adults.

Were a congregation to have two worship services on Sunday morning with an attendance ranging from 80 to 150 in one service and 170 to 240 in the other, it would definitely make sense to have two major adult choirs. Certainly if these two worship services were held in two separate buildings several miles apart, each would have its own choir. Just because the two services are held in the same building does not mean a church can "get away with" having just one choir. When that is done, one of the two services inevitably suffers from neglect.

Some of us can remember the days when the youth choir was used as the main choir for the first service on

Sunday morning. In a few congregations that may still work. Today it is not reasonable to ask the youth choir to be the anchor for the early service. The youth choir is appropriately called on to sing on specific, special occasions rather than to provide the music for one worship service on a regular weekly basis.

It works best to have two major adult choirs—or three, if you have three services. A few people may sing in both worship services on Sunday morning. That's fine. What is not helpful is for the choir to sing for the first service, stay through church school, and be in the second service just long enough to sing the anthem. As they leave, they create a vacuum that cannot be filled for the rest of the service.

It's a mistake to assume that having one choir director means having one adult choir. Feel free to have a specific, distinctive choir director for each worship service. He or she can be part-time or volunteer. Adult choirs are decisive in leading the service of worship.

Special Vocal Music

In some congregations, one of the best possibilities for growing forward dynamic, inspirational music is through solos and ensembles. This special music can, in exceptional ways, advance and strengthen the spirit of the service.

Take care that the number of solos or ensembles isn't overdone. They are perhaps most helpful during worship on the major community Sundays the church shares across the year.

The choir director who has coaching competencies has less need for paid soloists. The choir director who has neither the coaching competencies nor the time to help people improve their voices frequently tries to fall back on help from paid soloists and ensembles.

From time to time you may employ a paid soloist or a paid ensemble. I encourage you to invest these funds more wisely in a choir director with excellent coaching competencies. Such a choir director will reach out to, attract, and develop a network of volunteers who can share excellent special music. Over the long term, you'll be able to offer a wider range of music provided by a stronger core of persons involved in the music and the church.

Instrumentalists

One important way to strengthen the worship service is through individual instrumentalists, small groups, a band, an orchestra, or handbells. Each of these provides a way for persons to contribute their musical gifts to the service of worship and to share their instrumental strengths and competencies.

Indeed, in some congregations the service of worship is led by a small instrumental group. Others have their music led by a band or an orchestra. A focal point in some music programs is the handbell choir. I encourage you to draw on the resources of people who, across the years, have learned to play an instrument and who would be happy to contribute their gift individually or in a group.

Children's Choirs

Children's choirs are particularly significant in our time. Many public education facilities, for lack of funds, are having to cut back on music. Often this leaves children in the community dependent on the music they learn through the children's choirs at church.

Many children also discover the Christian faith well before confirmation time—in their Sunday school and in their children's choirs.

I encourage congregations to develop children's choirs. Helping children learn to sing and learn to love to sing is a wonderful gift they will enjoy throughout their life. Help them learn to sing the rich message of the Christian gospel. That is a message they will carry throughout their life.

Youth Choirs

The stronger the children's choirs, the more likely there will be a strong youth choir. There was a time when youth choirs were extraordinarily strong in this country. Youth choirs have not necessarily fallen by the wayside. Many congregations still have strong youth choirs. They have choir directors who share music young people like to sing.

Do youth choirs sing music written in this century and the last century? Yes. Do they learn some of the music written across the first, second, and third centuries? Yes. Do they sing music written in this generation that helps them understand the Christian life in this time? Yes.

Youth today have many demands on their time, and it's not easy to build a youth choir. Young people have a strong need to belong, to be part of a group. The art is to build a youth choir that helps them discover a sense of family, a sense of the Christian gospel, a sense of belonging to and contributing to the Christian mission. These are youth choirs that are strong and vital.

Special Choirs

Another way to enhance your church's music program is to form special choirs. There might be a special choir just for the summer, a different special choir just for the Advent season or for Holy Week services. Some congregations have a summer gospel hymn concert or a musical program associated with a patriotic holiday. Some do cantatas and oratorios.

There are at least two good reasons for special choirs; the first relates to time commitments. Due to jobs that require travel, young children at home, irregular work hours, and other pressures of our time, many people are unable to commit to long-term weekly choir responsibilities. They can often find time for a short-term special choir.

The second reason relates to the fact that many persons are excellent sprinters—they're at their best doing short-term, highly intensive projects with close deadlines. When you have special choirs, you give these excellent sprinters a significant opportunity to participate in a short-term musical project.

Each year you'll begin to build core groupings of persons who, on a regular basis from one year to the next, will participate in your church's special choirs, whether they're children's, youth, or adult choirs. Consider what special choirs would be helpful during the coming several years.

Another advantage to having special choirs is that the more people you get to participate in them, the more people you'll have who are likely, at some point, to participate in ongoing choirs. Some people in your special choirs may discover such a compelling sense of community and joy in music that they decide to be part of an ongoing choir. Still, a special choir has its own integrity and is not assembled for the purpose of getting more people into the ongoing choirs.

Festivals and Community Events

A further possibility for enhancing the music of your congregation is to participate in a community musical event or a music festival. A musical event in the community offers opportunities to establish relationships with unchurched persons. The nature and focus of these events varies considerably from one community to the next. Whatever form they take, the music of the congregation and the music of the choirs is frequently grown forward as they participate together in these festivals.

Retreats and Resource Leaders

An excellent possibility for growing the music in your congregation is through annual choir retreats and special resource leaders. Actually, these two go hand in hand. Many choirs who hold an annual choir retreat invite a resource leader to come and work with them for that brief but intensive, good fun, good times retreat.

Many choir members look forward to the retreat as one of the highlights of the year. They enjoy fellowship, recreation, and fun as they share together as a choir family. They also engage in many hours of concentrated, vigorous work in rehearsal as they prepare music for the coming season with the help of the visiting resource leader, their choir director, and the accompanist.

Look ahead. Consider which resource persons can best help advance the music of your choirs. Invite them to be with you, one after the other, over the coming several years. You will be helping your choirs and choir directors to grow.

Keyboard Music

Another way to strengthen your music in worship is through the contribution of a piano, a synthesizer, and/or an organ.

In many congregations, the instrument that weaves the service together is the piano, played by a gifted person. Many people sing at their best accompanied by a piano.

In recent times many congregations have begun to use synthesizers. They offer a broad range of musical possibilities. Indeed, in the coming years there will likely be more innovative, new instruments—beyond the synthesizer—from which congregations will benefit, just as they benefited centuries ago from the introduction of those new instruments the piano and the organ.

Whether your congregation has an electronic or a pipe organ (and there is considerable discussion about the merits of each), it can be an excellent instrument for setting the appropriate tone in the worship service. A skilled organist can draw a range of responses from the congregation—triumph, celebration, joy, serenity, prayerfulness—any of which are appropriate, depending on the focus of the service.

CHOOSING THE RESOURCES
THAT SUIT YOUR CONGREGATION

The eleven major music resources we've just discussed are to some extent listed in their order of strength and value. Churches with inspiring congregational singing do well, and many worship services focus primarily on this strength. Vital adult choirs will also certainly enhance your worship services; and, what is more, those who participate in these choirs will branch out and volunteer to help with vocal music, a children's choir, a youth choir, a special choir, and so on.

This is not necessarily to suggest the order in which you develop these resources. Pick whichever six you can best achieve and grow them forward. Your worship services will do extraordinarily well in helping people to worship God.

One fact worth noting is that a certain size sanctuary invites a certain size choir. This principle is also true of the piano, the synthesizer, and the organ. Some people focus first on fitting the instruments, rather than the choir, to the sanctuary. Yet it makes no sense to have a forty-rank pipe organ and a fifteen-voice choir. If the sanctuary is large enough to need a forty-rank instrument, it also needs a forty- to sixty-voice choir. Build the choirs first; then build the organ, should it makes sense to have one.

Look forward to developing six possibilities from the list of eleven that will best help you. Sometimes congregations become preoccupied with an organ. As a matter of fact, there are ten other music possibilities that will help you grow forward the strength of music in your congregation. The organ is the last possibility listed, not the first. Pick the six you can do best, go ahead, move forward, and make a joyful noise!

It's worth noting that the first ten possibilities include groupings of people. It will be more helpful to your congregation's long-range future to develop many groupings that contribute to the worship services than to fall back into dependency on one person who plays the piano, the synthesizer, or the organ. The more people you involve, the more people you help.

The instruments are intended to accompany the congregation and the choirs. It's not helpful for pianists or organists to behave as though the congregation and the choirs were supposed to accompany them.

I teach congregations to concentrate most of their best energies on the first ten possibilities. If the piano, the synthesizer, and/or the organ are among their best six possibilities, I urge them to concentrate some of their remaining energy on those after attending to the other five. Put first things first. Strong choirs will grow a strong organ. When a congregation has strong choirs, it certainly is able also to have whatever size organ makes sense. On the other hand, having a strong organ does not automatically grow strong choirs.

Yes, I have helped many congregations to acquire an excellent organ. At the same time, it is important to remember that having an organ is not a prerequisite to being an effective church. The church can be the church without an organ. The first-century church did well. The twenty-first century church will do well—and many of the strong, healthy congregations of the present and the future will do well without an organ. An organ is the eleventh possibility, not the first.

KEEPING AN EYE ON THE FUTURE

One of the best things you can do is to look several years ahead. Consider all eleven music possibilities. Decide which six you will focus on during the coming three to five years.

It's not necessary to focus on all six for the full duration. You might decide that in the coming two years you'll focus on developing children's choirs; in the third year you'll focus on developing instrumentalists.

Yes, the children's choirs will continue beyond those two years. And yes, the instrumentalists will play beyond year three; but you have a specific time period you set aside to grow a basic team of instrumentalists. From then on, that basic team will both serve as the instrumental resource for one of your worship services and discover new persons to be part of the team. You might decide that in the first year you'll focus on congregational singing and in the third year you're going to begin to hold annual choir retreats, bringing in resource leaders.

Develop a work-flow plan of how you're going to grow forward the six possibilities that will help best during the coming several years. As you achieve your goals, your worship will become increasingly dynamic and inspiring.

7:

Music and Mission

MISSION AND THE WORLD

Music is mission. The choir is mission. In a mission field, the music of the congregation is mission music. In a mission field, the choirs of the congregation share the mission.

God is in the world. Whenever the church's music is in the world, God is in the music. Whenever the church's music is not in the world, God is in the world. God is faithful to God's mission.

Think of each of your services of worship. Ask yourself these key questions:

- Does the music lead persons to share in the mission or to stay "inside" the church?
- Does the music help people with their foundational life searches—the quest for individuality, community, meaning, and hope?
- Does the music share the spirit of good news and the empowerment of resurrection?
- Does the music lead people to hope and a constructive future?

On a mission field, *mission* music is more helpful than church music. In a "mission music program" two important results occur:

- the music and the choirs inspire the congregation to go out and share in the mission, and

- the choirs themselves go out and share in the mission.

I am for church music. I grew up participating in a graded choir program that was among the best children's choir programs in the country. I learned much of the Christian life and faith singing in one choir after another in that extraordinary church music program.

Today what is needed is a mission music program more than a "churched" music program. The children, youth, and adults are given the words and the music with which to share the Christian mission in and with the community and the world. One of the best things a choir does is to be a mission choir.

SUGGESTIONS ABOUT MUSIC STYLE

Some people have yet to discover the possibility of "mission music." Some hold out for what they call traditional music. Others advocate what they call contemporary music; still others cherish gospel music.

Those who hold out for traditional music tend to insist on "quality" music, asserting that church music standards must be maintained. Their point on quality is well taken. These further points help:

- What some now call traditional music was really pioneering and innovative in its own time.

- Some of the traditional music can help to advance the congregation's participation in the mission.

- Some persons in the community are, in fact, reached for Christ through traditional music.
- Traditional music does not have a monopoly on quality; there is quality in some contemporary and some gospel music as well.

Those interested in church growth frequently advocate contemporary music, insisting that this is the only way to get new members. They make a good point—this is no longer a churched culture. These further points help:

- God calls us to mission growth. If membership growth happens as well, that is a happy by-product. Sometimes we are too preoccupied with increasing the membership inside the institution. We are called to share the mission in the world.
- Some so-called contemporary music is gimmicky and trivial; what people long for is help with their foundational life searches.
- Too much of contemporary music focuses "inside" the church.

People who cherish gospel music suggest this is the best way to reach persons for Christ. They have an important understanding—music can reach persons for Christ. These further points help:

- Traditional and contemporary music can reach persons for Christ as well.
- Gospel music is sometimes too preoccupied with the cross; the best gospel music can help persons discover the resurrection and the risen Lord.
- Some gospel music tends toward legalism and law; the best gospel music shares grace and compassion.

In the final analysis, too much of the whole discussion—traditional versus contemporary versus gospel music—is an "inside-the-church" discussion. Traditionalists seek to protect their turf, and membership growth advocates try to get more members. Gospelists insist that their music will save the day.

The truth is that the discussion needs to move toward increasing the mission, not perpetuating, increasing, or saving the church. The discussion needs to focus on the mission more than the church. The discussion needs to become more preoccupied with advancing the mission and less concerned with the institution. All three camps need to focus more fully on the mission. That is where the future is.

The truth is that some traditional, some contemporary, and some gospel music

- does lead persons to the mission rather than staying "inside" the church;
- does help people with their foundational life searches for individuality, community, meaning, and hope;
- does share the spirit of good news and the power of resurrection;
- docs lead people to hope and a constructive future.

The truth is that new forms of music, yet unknown, will emerge to help advance the mission. God has not finished with us. God will lead us to new expressions of music that stir the soul and inspire the mission. These are the important truths that will help advance the future of mission music programs.

MISSION MUSIC AND CHURCHED MUSIC

The key dynamic is between mission music and churched music. To be sure, certain pieces of churched music help with the mission. At the same time, whenever the music focuses primarily inside the church, it is less helpful for our time, or, for that matter, for any time.

Music that helps people discover the mission is music that has real spirit and power. Some of this will be classical, some gospel, and some contemporary. The test is not whether it is one kind of music or another. The test is whether the music focuses persons inside the church or advances the mission outside the church. The test is whether the music leads people to mission.

In a churched culture it was possible for the music to remain focused inside the church and for choirs to sing primarily inside the church. Going to church was a widely accepted practice, and many people sought out the church on their own initiative. Because a great proportion of the population participated in church, it was natural for choirs to sing primarily in church.

On rare occasions a choir might have visited and sung at a nursing home or a hospital. When they went on tour, they sang in churches. The primary focus of both their music and their activity was inside the church.

In a mission field, the music leads the congregation to the mission, and, equally important, the choirs invest some of their best energy in mission in the community. They might sing in a vocational setting or for a civic gathering. It might be in a factory, an office, a civic auditorium.

Some choirs participate in a mission project such as Habitat for Humanity and in the midst of that sing in community events to the glory of God. When they go on tour, they sing in mission settings more than inside-the-church settings. Inside some churches, yes, and yet more in mission settings.

Some choirs participate regularly, not occasionally, in programs at prisons, hospitals, schools, inner-city community centers, shopping malls, and office buildings. It is not something they do only at Christmas; they do these mission activities periodically and regularly across the year. The music and the choirs advance the mission.

GAUGING THE MUSIC'S SPIRIT AND POWER

As I mentioned earlier, people have four foundational life searches:

- The search for individuality
- The search for community
- The search for meaning
- The search for hope

People are drawn to music whose words and melody help them to discover some fulfillment in these four foundational life searches. Music that does this has spirit and power.

It is important to note that both the words *and* the melody have spirit and power. It is not simply that the tune has spirit and the words have power. The tune has power as well. People frequently hum a tune. Even when they can't quite remember the words, the melody and the memory bring back to them a sense of hope and joy during the tough, tight times of life.

Extraordinary musicians from earlier centuries created hymns with tunes and words of significance and power for that time and place. It is important that we discover those hymns and benefit from them. What I would also like you to see is that, in our time, it will be helpful to create hymns with new words and new melodies that have spirit and power for this time and place. Each generation fashions hymns, praise songs, and choruses that have spirit and power for that generation.

As we enter the twenty-first century, it's important to realize that we're not bound by some trade-off between traditional, contemporary, and gospel music. Each style includes specific pieces of music that can stir and strengthen us. It is the music itself, not the category, that is endowed with spirit and power. When the words and melody help us with our foundational life searches, we know the music has achieved its purpose.

HYMNS THAT SHARE THE GOOD NEWS

The gospel is good news, not bad news. People are helped by hymns, anthems, choruses, and praise songs that share good news, that share grace and peace, compassion and community, encouragement and vision, confidence and hope.

People are not helped by music that is mournful and gloomy or that focuses solely on the experience of the cross. People are helped by music that lives and shares the message of resurrection.

We are the Easter people, not only people of the cross. The event did not end on the cross. For all the hymns that focus on the cross, we need twice as many that focus on the resurrection, the risen Lord, and new life in Christ.

Our confidence is in the risen Lord. The disciples looked back on the crucifixion after having experienced the resurrection. It is true that Christ died on the cross because he loved us. It is also true that Jesus as the living, risen Lord loves us.

As we approach the twenty-first century, we need a theology of hope and hymns and music that reflect that theology. That is what will resonate well in the mission field God has given us.

FOCUSING ON THE PRESENT AND THE FUTURE

We are a pioneer people. We are a pilgrimage people. The most decisive understanding of God in the Old Testament is of the God who goes before us, as a cloud by day and a fire by night, leading us toward that future that God has both promised and prepared for us.

The most decisive image of God in the New Testament is disclosed by the open tomb, the risen Lord, and new life

in Christ. We can't live in the past; it is over and done. There
are only two things we can do about the past: (1) We can
give thanks to God for the accomplishments and achieve-
ments of the past; and (2) We can ask God's forgiveness for
the sins of omission and commission that we have done. We
cannot change what has been.

We can do something with the future. People new to
our congregation cannot participate in the past. Indeed,
none of us can participate in the past. What is done is done.
Congregations that live in the past don't attract new people.
Congregations that live in the present and the future reach
new people in the name of Christ.

I encourage you to develop music that focuses in pioneering ways on the present and the future. Yes, we will also
continue to sing many of the old hymns, especially those
with a pioneering vision of the future.

A sociologist once did an interesting study in Ap-
palachia. He concluded that the pioneers who cut the trees
and built the log cabins lived with a confident sense of hope
that they were building a new and promised land. He also
concluded that their descendants now eke out a bare, mea-
ger, desperate existence with no sense of hope.

In his research, the one place the sociologist failed to
visit were the white clapboard churches up on the ridges
and down in the hollows to listen to the hymns being sung.
On Sunday morning he would have heard these hymns: "We
Shall Gather at the River," "Dwelling in Beulah Land," "In
the Sweet By and By." These are not hymns of the past;
these are hymns of hope for the future.

To be sure, the hope may be postponed to the next
life—beyond the river—but those hymns look forward, not
back. When people cannot see their hopes being realized in
the present or the immediate future or the distant future,
they postpone their hopes down the road to the next life beyond the river. People live on hope more than on memory.

I'm not suggesting that we give up all of our old music. I'm suggesting that much of the music we now think of as historical was actually pioneering in its time, and in its time it focused on the future.

Let us give thanks for the best of what has been and move forward with music that helps us have a pioneering sense of the future, a sense of the future that God calls us toward in mission. This spirit in music will bless the mission of your congregation.

Let the music of your worship services

- lead persons to the mission rather than staying inside the church;
- help people with their foundational life searches of individuality, community, meaning, and hope;
- share the spirit of good news and the power of resurrection;
- lead people to hope and a constructive future.

Music focused on mission helps the church move forward in mission. Music focused only on the church does not help the church to be in mission. Sing, play, and live the music that helps your congregation to be in mission.

PART THREE:

ADDING POWER AND MOVEMENT TO WORSHIP

8:

Worship Services with Less Inertia and More Momentum

The third component that helps worship to be corporate and dynamic, stirring and inspiring, helpful and hopeful is the power and movement of the service. Here are eight hallmarks of a powerful service of worship that conveys a sense of progress—of starting, journeying, and arriving. A service that succeeds in this respect

- communicates strength and grace
- launches people forward into a new week
- focuses on human hope and confidence
- holds together well, with its various parts connected, and embraces spontaneity
- takes its mission and purpose seriously
- spends as much time celebrating new life and blessings and looking to the future as it does memorializing losses

- focuses on the whole person, offering a balance between the simple and the complex, the emotional and the intellectual
- has an order of service that helps people in their foundational life searches

Let me explore these characteristics here with you more fully.

STRENGTH AND GRACE OF THE SERVICE

Some worship services are like a car with a nearly-dead battery on a cold morning: They crank and die, crank and die, crank and die, and then slowly get chugging along. The only thing that the organ prelude, the call to worship, and the opening hymn have in common is that they happen at about the same point in the galaxy and usually on a Sunday morning. Although these three elements follow one another, there is no perceptible connection, nothing builds from one to the next. The service almost gets started, then almost gets started, then almost gets started. If it gets going at all, it chugs along feebly.

Thankfully there are many services of worship that begin strong and stay strong, and as the service moves forward, it conveys a sense of grace. Services like these lead people closer to the presence of God. They experience the strength of God in their life. They experience the grace of God surrounding their life.

THE FIRST DAY AS GATEWAY TO THE WEEK AHEAD

You can sense that a worship service has power and movement when the key leaders, the choir, the choir director, the accompanist, and the pastor communicate the spirit that worship happens on the first day of the week. When people share this conviction, these three things happen:

- The service is among the best, most well-prepared events in the life of the congregation and the whole community.
- The service looks forward to the days ahead and helps people to launch the week before them.
- The service is the worship of the Easter people.

We are essentially a "first day of the week" people. It was on the first day of the week that some women walked to a tomb and discovered that the stone had been rolled away and that the Lord had risen.

I have attended a few worship services where it was clear that the key leaders, the choir, the choir director, the accompanist, and the pastor all shared the perspective that worship happens on the last day of the week. When the underlying assumption is that the week begins on Monday, then Sunday's worship is viewed as happening on the last day of the week. Three things happen:

- "Last day of the week" services of worship are among the least well-prepared events in the congregation.
- The service looks back on the week that was and functions as a summary of what has been.
- The focus of the worship tends to stay on the cross and hardly ever discovers Easter.

Regrettably, there are pastors who have been so influenced by the culture that they think their week begins on Monday when they go to their office.

The week begins on Sunday, not Monday. It begins on Sunday with the people of God—the Easter people—worshiping God. It does not begin on Monday in an office with staff meetings and stacks of paper.

Now, it's true that we all need help with what has been: There is much for which we need to ask God's forgiveness; there is much for which we can give God thanks and praise. And yet what has been has been, and we can do nothing to change it. What we *can* do something with is what will be.

Most people go to a service of worship not to look back but to look forward. What keeps most of us lying awake at night is not what has been but what might be. The service of worship that happens on the last day of the week tends to neglect helping people with the week to come.

The worship service planned and prayed for from the perspective that it is happening on the first day of the week is the service of worship that launches people into the week ahead. It gives guidance for the choices they will be making in the future.

HOPE AND CONFIDENCE

Worship services have power and movement when the service conveys the conviction that we are a people of hope and confidence. We have an abiding trust in the future God is preparing for us.

In some services of worship, all the prayers are continually focused on who is sick and dying. It almost becomes the refrain of the service. That preoccupation confirms once again for us, and teaches every first-time worshiper, that we are a congregation primarily focused on sickness and dying—that we are a sick and dying congregation.

Life *is* a matter of sickness and dying, and when we are suffering, we count on the prayers of the people to help us through. At the same time, life is also a matter of hope and confidence—now and beyond illness and death.

Indeed, some congregations pray for a sick person, and then when the person gets well, they don't even stop to rejoice in that recovery; they simply move on to the next person who is sick and dying!

It is not helpful to become preoccupied with illness and death in our services of worship. It is vital to maintain our focus on a sense of hope and a spirit of confidence. As the people of hope, we live in the confidence that we are the people whom God goes before as a cloud by day and a fire by night, leading us to that future that God has promised and prepared for us. We are the people of the risen Lord. We are the people who have new life in Christ.

With the dynamics of hope and confidence the worship service is fully one of power and movement.

CONNECTING THE PARTS
AND ENCOURAGING SPONTANEITY

A service of worship that has power and movement is a service with integrity and spontaneity. Integrity means that the service holds together well. It is of whole cloth. It has a sense of unity, of being connected. The music, the liturgy, and the preaching support one another and build on one another.

When a service of worship is disconnected, one event follows another, but it's not clear whether those events stand alone or build on each other toward one purpose. There is no sense of wholeness. It is as though the music, the liturgy, and the preaching are three distinctive tracks that happen one after another in the same space.

A service of worship with power and movement has a sense of wholeness and connectedness. People leave having had an experience of enduring value, purpose, and significance.

These services also have a sense of spontaneity; the service is not dull and routine. Some services are so aimless and boring that one sometimes wonders if even God has trouble concentrating. To be sure, God *is* always present, and God is richly present in those services that have integrity and spontaneity.

It is interesting that the more integrity the service has, the more spontaneity the service has also. Services that lack integrity tend to be tense and tight, rigid and ritualistic. Services that have a sense of integrity, a sense of purpose, a sense of direction are freer also to enjoy a sense spontaneity.

I remember Glen Johnson well. He is among the best, most competent, most devoted ministers of music I have ever known. His compassion and sense of mission have been inspiring. He would work very intentionally to help the service have a sense of integrity, purpose, and direction. The service would be well planned in advance, well thought through, and well prayed for. It was precisely because of this that the worship leaders, the director of the music, and the pastor felt free to bring a spirit of spontaneity to the service.

Glen would prayerfully and devotedly listen to the pastoral prayer, and as soon as he sensed the spirit of that particular prayer he would select one of the several choral responses the choir knew by heart. He would communicate his choice to the choir by a subtle signal—few in the congregation knew that the choral response that always seemed to be so well matched to the prayer had been selected only moments before.

Likewise, Glen listened thoughtfully to the sermon, and then he would spontaneously select the best closing hymn (it was intentionally not selected in advance) to help the congregation to sing the message of the morning. Throughout the service, Glen would be praying and reflecting on what choral response to the benediction would weave together the whole of the service and send people forward with a sense of grace, of strength, and of mission and confidence.

These are three simple efforts on the part of an excellent director of music to weave the service together with a sense of spontaneity and relevance during the course of the service. And because the service of worship had such a sense of well-planned integrity, the worship leaders, the director of the music, the pastor felt free to move through the service in ways not fully planned. It is most helpful to be open to the movement of the Spirit of God in a service of worship.

We can confess to God that some services of worship are so lifeless, so dreary and dull, that we don't even nudge our dozing neighbor. At least they'll benefit from a moment of rest and leave refreshed because of that short nap.

People don't nod and doze through a service that has integrity and spontaneity. People have a sense of expectancy. Energy is in the air. People come anticipating the ways in which God will touch their life in this service.

With the integrity of solid preparation and the spontaneity to respond to unexpected opportunities, the worship service has power and movement.

MISSION AND PURPOSE

On the threshold of the twenty-first century, we are in a situation much like the first century. This is a mission field; this is not a churched culture. In our time, worship services with power and movement are those that take seriously the age of mission, take seriously the mission field in which God has planted us.

Services of worship that don't have power and movement may be built on the naive assumption that this is still a churched culture. Such services focus on maintenance and institution; they have a functional and organizational orientation and are primarily preoccupied with the survival of a church that is not growing or that is dying.

Mission congregations are primarily preoccupied with their mission and purpose. Their services of worship have a strong spirit of direction and reinforce the congregation's dedication to give of itself in the community and across the planet. Mission congregations live with two equally important convictions:

- Mission is worship

- Worship is mission

It's hard for persons and congregations who have a church-culture, organizational, institutional mind-set to understand the close proximity of mission and worship, worship and mission. They tend to divide the two, as if they could be placed in different compartments: Mission is what we do out there; worship is what we do in here.

Persons and congregations who discover the mission and purpose to which God calls them understand that when they are in mission, they are indeed worshiping God. We live in one of the richest ages for mission that God has ever given the church. To share the mission is to worship God. In sharing the mission we do so with a deep sense of reverence and worship.

Persons and congregations who discover the mission and purpose to which God calls them understand how urgent and necessary their need for worship is. They understand that what they don't need is poorly done, uninspiring, dull, and institutionally preoccupied services of worship. The depth of their mission needs the strength of worship. The quality of their mission needs worship services that

- focus on the mission, not the institution; and

- reinfuse them with the vitality and hope they need to deliver even more richly and fully the mission to which God is calling them.

CELEBRATING BLESSINGS AND LOOKING
TO THE FUTURE

The dynamics of celebration and looking to the future help a service of worship to have power and movement. Overinvesting in memorializing the past takes away from a service's power and movement. Underinvesting in celebration and future does the same.

I once attended a Sunday morning worship that included a memorial service in which the congregation, once a year, remembered all those who had died during the previous year. At one point in the service the pastor thoughtfully read the name of each person who had died. As the names were read, the organ played softly in the background, and outside, the church bell tolled slowly. The service climaxed with a prayer of thanksgiving for those lives and a hymn of victory.

Afterward, when the pastor asked me what I thought of the service, I told him, "It was excellent, most helpful, most meaningful." Then I asked him, "When do you do the same for each new baby born this past year, for each person who has discovered Christ during this past year, and for those who have significantly advanced God's mission during this past year?"

"Oh," he replied. "Well, when a baby is born, we place a rose on the altar."

I said, "Yes. One rose, one service. And when a person dies, you often have flowers on the altar from the funeral service, and people take food over to help the family in the midst of their grief. You offer prayer for the person and the family during the illness; then you offer prayer for them on the Sunday following the funeral service. You do all these things for those experiencing grief at the end of a life. And you do this excellent memorial service once a year. You are celebrating the past. Celebrate the future as well."

Should you choose to have a worship service honoring those who have died, be certain also to have a service celebrating the new life of those who have been born. Pray for those who are born and their families and friends who are experiencing the beginning of life. Have a service to celebrate with the persons who have discovered Christ during this past year. Have a service to celebrate with those who have significantly advanced God's mission during this past year.

Pray for those new to this human life, for those new to a life in Christ, for those who are advancing the mission. Help your services of worship focus equally as much on celebration and the future as on sorrow and the past. When you do this, your services of worship will resonate with power and movement.

FINDING A BALANCE
FOR THE WHOLE PERSON

Power and movement are present when the whole service touches the whole person with the whole gospel. While helping one congregation, I consulted with their minister of music, one of the most widely respected church music directors in the United States. As we talked, he said to me, "Dr. Callahan, I have had more complaints about the music in the past six months than in the prior ten years with this congregation."

As we talked, I took a sheet of paper and drew a spectrum, and on one end of the spectrum I put the words *simple, stirring, inspiring, emotional*. On the other end of the spectrum I put the words *complex, profound, thoughtful, intellectual*. Figure 8.1 shows the finished diagram.

I told him, "Look at this diagram. Some music is simple, stirring, inspiring, and emotional. Some music is complex, profound, thoughtful, and intellectual. Think about

Figure 8.1

simple	complex
stirring	profound
inspiring	thoughtful
emotional	intellectual

the past six months and tell me where the range of music in the services of worship has been."

He thought about the preludes, postludes, choruses, anthems, and hymns and decided that during this time the music had covered all parts of the spectrum. However, on perhaps eight of twelve Sundays the music tended to edge a bit toward the complex, profound, thoughtful, intellectual end of the spectrum (please see figure 8.2).

Gradually a clear assessment of the situation dawned on me. During the prior ten years, the pastor's preaching tended (on eight out of twelve Sundays) toward the simple, stirring, inspirational, emotional side of the spectrum. Combined with the music that was more complex and profound, the service had a sense of balance (please see figure 8.3), and

Figure 8.2

	music	
simple		complex
stirring		profound
inspiring		thoughtful
emotional		intellectual

Figure 8.3

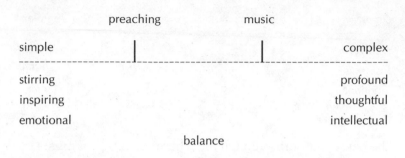

this balance had been present for ten years. There was a sense that the whole service touched the whole person.

Then, about six months before I visited, a new pastor arrived. His preaching tended to be more toward the complex, profound, thoughtful, intellectual side of the spectrum than the music was. The service had lost its former sense of balance, as the diagram in figure 8.4 shows.

The new pastor used long, complicated, difficult sentences. The former pastor's sentences were short. The new pastor used many parenthetical expressions in the middle of sentences, and if you missed the parenthetical expression, you didn't get the point of the sentence.

The former pastor's sentences were clear and simple, using nickel-and-dime words. The new pastor had come from an intellectual college community, and he used fifty-dollar and hundred-dollar words. His sentences sounded something like this: "The eschatological significance of this soteriological text has ontological value as we look at the sociological trends of the times."

During the new pastor's first six months, people left the service feeling that something was not quite the same. They thought it surely could not be the fault of this learned, impressive new pastor, so they concluded it must therefore have something to do with the music.

Figure 8.4

	music	preaching	
simple						complex

stirring			profound
inspiring			thoughtful
emotional			intellectual

I told the director of music, "Good friend, from today
forward, I count on you to see to it that the music—eight
out of twelve Sundays is toward the simple, stirring, inspiring, and emotional side of the spectrum." The diagram
in figure 8.5 depicts this approach.

I went on to say, "Yes, I am aware that you, as a minister of music, are rigid, stubborn, inflexible, have high musical standards, and have a national reputation at stake.
And amid your rigidity and inflexibility, I count on your
creativity to get you to the simple side of the spectrum for
eight out of twelve Sundays. There are classical pieces that
are simple, stirring, and inspiring and that touch the heart.
Sing those. The other four out of twelve Sundays, feel free
to sing anything else you want."

Figure 8.5

	music		preaching	
simple						complex

stirring			profound
inspiring			thoughtful
emotional			intellectual

balance

We need to create a sense of balance in our worship services. It's important that the whole service touch the whole person with the whole gospel.

This does not mean a trade-off between traditional music and contemporary music or contemporary music and gospel music. Some traditional music is simple, stirring, inspiring, and emotional, just as some traditional music is complex, profound, thoughtful, and intellectual. Some contemporary music is simple and emotional, and some is complex and intellectual. The same variety can be found in gospel pieces.

Another way to help touch the whole person is to intentionally balance the music with the sermon. When the sermon is intended to be a teaching sermon, provide music that is simple and stirring, that touches the heart. When the sermon is meant primarily to be inspiring, feel free to plan music that is slightly more complex and profound.

Keep this understanding foremost: In a mission field, the tone of worship, in order to reach unchurched persons, should tend more toward simplicity and inspiration. Consider Easter, Christmas, your major community Sundays, and your new services of worship as they would be seen through the eyes of an unchurched person. Help these services to be less like advanced trigonometry and more like basic math. Help it to be more like a first-century service.

It took the Christian church fifteen hundred years to develop some of the complexities of our worship services. And it has taken Protestant congregations nearly five hundred years since the Reformation in 1517 to build further on that and to develop complexities of worship that one could probably get away with in a churched culture.

In a mission field—in southern China, central India, northern Africa, Central or South America, or in Australia or North America—we do best to have a service of worship that is more toward the simple, rather than the complex, side of the spectrum.

Be at peace about this. This isn't a trade-off between contemporary services on the one hand and traditional services on the other. You can have a high liturgical service of worship that is simple and stirring. It is not necessarily the case that all high liturgical services need to be complex, profound, and intellectual.

We go to a worship service expecting our deepest yearnings and longings to be stirred. We count on the service to touch our heart and stir our soul. We look forward to having our understanding of everyday life thoughtfully and profoundly advanced in the light of the gospel.

Think less in terms of traditional versus contemporary, traditional versus gospel. Think less in terms of low-church contemporary and high-church ritualistic. These categories have their own value elsewhere.

Think with a new set of categories. Is this worship service simple, stirring, inspiring, and emotional? Traditional, contemporary, and gospel services can be. Is this service complex, profound, thoughtful, and intellectual? Some traditional, contemporary, and gospel services are.

Ask yourself, Is this a service with a sense of balance? Does it inspire? Is the service profound and thoughtful? Are people's longings stirred? Is their understanding of day-to-day life advanced in the light of the gospel? Does the whole service touch the whole person with the whole gospel? Worship services that touch the whole person with the whole Gospel have tremendous power and movement.

THE GOAL OF THE ORDER OF SERVICE

The eighth hallmark of a service of worship that has power and movement is the presence of an order of service that helps persons with their foundational life searches. Life is a pilgrimage and a search. As I mentioned in chapter 7, there are four foundational life searches:

- The search for individuality—that is, the search for identity, integrity, autonomy, power.
- The search for community—that is, the search for roots, place, belonging, sharing, and caring.
- The search for meaning—that is, the search for value, significance, purpose, and understanding in day-to-day life.
- The search for hope—that is, the search for a stable and reliable future.

In my book *Effective Church Leadership*, you will discover a chapter on each of the foundational life searches.

When people come to worship, they bring with them these foundational life searches. Think about how the order of service can help them begin to fulfill these foundational life searches. When you consider your various orders of service, ask yourself in what ways this specific order of service will help people with their search for individuality, community, meaning, and hope.

Just as there is a diversity of gifts, there is a variety of orders of worship. Helpful orders of worship

- lead persons to the mission;
- help people with their foundational life searches of individuality, community, meaning, and hope;
- share the spirit of good news and the power of resurrection; and
- lead persons to a constructive future.

In order to accomplish these goals, your congregation will need more than one specific order of worship.

I've been intrigued by people who express concern that an order of service be "doctrinally correct." My experience has led me to conclude that the primary concern is in fact whether an order of service is helpful in people's life and destiny. I might gently suggest that on occasion—not always—a person insisting on a doctrinally correct order of service is actually insisting on a specific culture's order of service. It is easy to confuse our own cultural preferences with doctrinal correctness.

All of us bring to an order of service the culture, or cultures, in which we grew up and have lived. It would be nearly impossible to create an order of service that had no cultural orientation. What I'm suggesting is that the primary concern of an order of service is neither cultural commentary nor doctrinal correctness. The primary purpose of an order of service is to be helpful in people's life in the name of Christ.

In worship we give praise to God. We discover the richness of our individuality as a child of God. We discover who we are and whose we are as we give praise to God. We find an abiding sense of identity and integrity. We confess both our individual and our communal sinfulness, and we are drawn together as a community of faith, a confessing church. We discover our commonality, our roots, our place and belonging as God's pilgrim people in the movement of petition.

We discover the wisdom, insight, and grace of the Old and New Testaments. We learn to better understand the Christian mission across the centuries. This understanding gives our own lives new meaning—new significance and purpose—as we become part of the continuity of God's mission through time.

In worship we discover hope. We're not simply sent out as God's people. We're sent out as the people empowered by God for mission in the world. We are the people of hope. We are the Easter people. We are the people of Christmas. We are the people of wonder and joy, new life and resurrection.

What gives us a sense of enduring power is that we live in hope, not in memory. We remember well, and we hope even more fully.

As you consider your services of worship, look at these eight features we've discussed. Think through which of them you now have well in place. Of those there will be some that you can strengthen. Consider which ones you currently lack and would like to grow forward this coming year and which ones you'd like to focus on in the second year and the third year.

Develop five of these eight features well. When you select five of the eight and accomplish them, the other three will come along. When people try to build all eight, they end up not doing any of them very well.

Give yourself three years to cultivate the five features you can best develop. Then your services of worship will have power and movement and will lead people to sense the presence of God. Your services will send people forth with hope and mission.

PART FOUR:

WHEN WORSHIP SERVICES AND WORSHIP SPACES ARE COMPLEMENTARY

9:

Building a Range of Worship Options

A RECIPROCAL DYNAMIC

The reciprocal dynamic of the services and the sanctuary (or worship space) is the fourth component that helps worship to be corporate and dynamic, stirring and inspiring, helpful and hopeful. The services and the sanctuary go hand in hand. As you think about how they can best complement each other in your church, consider these six factors:

- The number of worship service options you offer
- The convenience of the options you offer
- The options that help "three-hour" persons
- The groupings you reach and help
- The realistic seating range of your sanctuary
- The new worship services you offer

By growing and developing any four of these six factors you'll advance the strength and helpfulness of your worship life as a congregation and you'll help and serve many people in your community. We'll discuss seating range in chapter 10 and adding new services in chapter 11. Let's focus now on the variety of services a church can offer.

WORSHIP SERVICE OPTIONS

The more options you offer, the more people you will help. I used to say that the more options you offer, the more people you will reach. This is still true. At the same time, I discovered some congregations then focused primarily on reaching people, as though that were the end in itself. They focused on the numbers reached rather than the quality of the help shared in worship. Our purpose in reaching people is to help them with their life and destiny.

The primary task, then, is not simply to reach people. It is to genuinely help persons grow and build their life. When the focus is on the strength and quality of the worship services, persons are reached and genuinely helped as they worship God.

Some congregations think they offer two services of worship. In fact they offer one strong, excellent service of worship, usually at eleven o'clock on Sunday morning. They also offer what they call an early service; in reality it's more like a warm-up practice for the "real" service at eleven o'clock.

In that early service there is little effort to be warm and winsome. Generally there are no new-person greeters. The service has no music of substance; there is usually a semi-willing soloist or a reluctant ensemble. The service has no full choir. The preaching comes off as a halting, warm-up practice. The early service's lack of power and movement is like the almost-dead battery on a cold winter morning that I described in chapter 8.

The people who come to that early service have a right to look forward to a full, rich service of worship, one that has quality and is well prepared and well prayed for. It is, after all, the only worship service in which they will participate this week. They're not necessarily looking for a service that is identical to the eleven o'clock service. They're looking for a strong service that helps them with the week to come.

Regrettably, most of those who plan an early service—music directors, worship leaders, and pastors—worship at 11:00. They don't regularly experience the early service and therefore fail to realize that it's often less well prepared and, many times, poorly done. If they do attend from time to time, they do so with the assumption that this is not the "main service." Then they wonder why fewer people come to the early service of worship.

There's a clue even in the names—"early service" and "main service." It's a matter of perspective. For those who come to the "early service," it is their *main* service. But from the vantage point of those who worship at eleven o'clock, it's an "early service" because, after all, the "main service" happens later.

Some churches confusingly refer to their 11:00 service as their "first service" because historically it was first. They refer to their 8:30 service as their "second service" because at some point in the past it was developed second. Many times it is a second-rate service as well.

This parochial perspective results in an early worship service that is less than a full service. It results in a service that lacks the central components of dynamic, shared worship.

A helpful way forward is to refer to each service simply by the time it is offered. It is not early or late, first or second. One says simply, "We have an eight-thirty worship service, and we have an eleven o'clock worship service."

Whatever options of worship you offer, it is important that they be strong and well done. They don't have to be the same; they don't have to be markedly dissimilar. It's not necessary that one service be a traditional service and the other a contemporary service. In that mix what frequently happens is that the contemporary service is poorly done—and the excuse for it being poorly done is that it is "contemporary."

A more helpful way to think of the options you offer is that some worship services are simple and other services are more complex. A simple service can be vibrant, as can a complex one.

The primary consideration has more to do with the "degree of difficulty" of the worship services and less to do with the categories of traditional and contemporary or of low church and high church. Many persons in the community, many new to the Christian life, many grassroots members of the congregation, and even many who are long-time Christians are helped by a *simple* service of worship.

In a given congregation, two services of worship may both be high church—one is simple, the other is more complex in its liturgical formulation. Complex is not more advanced or better; it is merely more complex.

The real key is to offer as many options as possible and to be certain that all the worship services are well planned and shared, with a constant dedication to helping persons worship God well.

CONVENIENCE

The more convenient the options, the more people you will help. Worship has always been at the most convenient time. The reason worship was at 11:00 A.M. in the early part of this century was because society was mostly agricultural.

Farmers had early morning chores. The trip to church was in a wagon or a buggy over rough roads. They had Sunday school first, and the reasonable and convenient time to worship was at eleven o'clock. If the farmers hadn't had animals to feed and other chores to do, they, like many people today, might have preferred to worship at an earlier time in order to spend more of the day with their families.

In many communities today, services at 8:30 or 9:00 A.M. are most convenient to unchurched couples with small children, unchurched single parents with small children, unchurched persons in their twenties and thirties, and unchurched people in early retirement. We are likely to reach and help more of these persons with a worship service at 8:30 or 9:00 A.M. than we are at 11:00 A.M..

Of course, were you to do a survey among families with small children in your church, they would teach you that 8:30 or 9:00 A.M. is too early for them. They may have preferred an earlier hour, but have adapted to the later hour. This is the wrong group to survey. Instead survey the unchurched groups just mentioned. They'll respond that children don't sleep in on Sunday morning. Indeed, children don't sleep in on any morning. They would prefer a worship service earlier so they could have more of the day for other family activities. For them, an eleven o'clock service splits the day too much. Remember, unchurched persons have never learned the "tradition" that God only shows up at 11:00 A.M.

"Ah," someone might say, "but if they were more committed, they would come to the eleven o'clock service, convenient or not." I would respond that most of these people are new to the Christian life; commitment develops over time.

Further, remember that many who come to the eleven o'clock service have learned the tradition that God really shows up then. And many who come to that service are there because for them it *is* the most convenient time.

Nothing in the New Testament suggests that God shows up only at eleven o'clock on Sunday morning. The New Testament does say that "where two or three are gathered together in my name, there I will be also."

The art is to think through the grouping you hope to help with each service of worship and then discover the most convenient worship time for that grouping. I work with congregations that have strong, excellent worship services at a variety of times:

- on Saturday afternoon at 4:00 in order to help young couples with school-age children;
- at 6:00 P.M. on Saturday evening to help persons whose pattern is to go to dinner and a late show;
- at 7:30 A.M. on Thursday morning to help those who are getting off the 11:00 P.M. to 7:00 A.M. work shift at the local medical facilities.

I've worked with congregations who discovered that many people were leaving after work on Friday for the mountains or seashore, and they therefore scheduled a worship service at 5:00 P.M. on Sunday to help them as they returned to town and launched the week to come.

There is no magic in any of these times. It takes wisdom and much thought on the part of a congregation to discover the most convenient times for different groupings and then to offer an excellent service of worship at those convenient time.

ACCOMMODATING "THREE-HOUR" PERSONS

Consider this fairly typical pattern: A family comes to worship at 9:30 A.M., during which time their children are in

Sunday school, and then goes home. We're inclined to think of them as one-hour persons because they are at one hour of worship. In fact they are three-hour persons.

Look at it through their eyes. They begin getting the children ready at eight, hoping to leave the house with some reasonable degree of sanity around nine. Sometimes one member of the family is already in the car gently tapping the horn and wondering where everybody else is. They drive to church, find a place to park, get the children to their Sunday school classrooms, and then share together in worship at 9:30. At 10:30 they don't rush off. They visit a little, collect their children, and return home around 11:00.

For them 8:00 to 11:00 represents a three-hour pattern. In a mission field, most people will start out as three-hour persons in their participation before they become four-and-a-half-hour persons. It takes some time before they change their pattern to both church school and worship, which involves a four-and-a-half-hour commitment (beginning the pilgrimage at 8:00 and returning home at 12:30).

Most people who have small children, even those who are churched, are also three-hour people until their children become slightly older and can make it for the longer stretch on Sunday mornings.

The more three-hour possibilities you offer, therefore, the more new people you are likely to help. The more you schedule your services so that the only option is four and a half hours, so that you try to force a four-and-a-half-hour participation, the fewer new people you will reach and help. Having worship and church school at the same time doesn't prevent people from participating in both. What it actually does is permit new persons to become three-hour people.

Once the new persons have become comfortable three-hour persons, the primary reason most of them become four-and-a-half-hour persons is because someone has been wise enough to start a new adult Sunday school class at the other hour. You may have people who have been coming to the 9:30 service of worship while their children have been in nursery, toddler, or kindergarten classes. As the children get older, the art is to start the new adult class either at 8:15 or 11:00.

People move to participating at the four-and-a-half-hour level because they are drawn to the new adult Sunday school class that further helps them develop a sense of roots, place and belonging, sharing and caring. If no one starts the new adult class at the other hour when the children are old enough, the parents continue to be three-hour people.

The research is very clear: People invest three hours for a good while before they invest four and a half. Give them a chance, and they will do well.

SCHEDULING SERVICES TO HELP PARTICULAR GROUPINGS

The more groupings you help, the stronger your mission. One of the best things you can do is to analyze the groupings you are now helping and which you have the potential to help.

A simple way to do this analysis is to look at the schedule of your services and determine who participates in the options you offer.

The charts included here will help you discover the groupings you are serving in worship. The schedules and the times given are merely illustrative and are not meant to impose any uniform standard. Your own schedules may differ, and that's fine.

Using the principles in the following charts, develop a chart that represents your current services. Focus on analyzing your own options. Discover the number of three-hour options and four-and-a-half-hour options that are available. Remember that the more three-hour options you offer, the more you'll help persons new to the Christian movement.

Consider ways you can serve more persons in worship. The charts include a line beside each grouping where you can indicate the number of persons in that grouping. You'll also find it helpful to make notes on the chart describing the nature of each grouping.

As figure 9.1 indicates, the congregation that is offering church school followed by worship on Sunday morning is helping three distinctive groupings of persons. Group 1 includes the people—youth and adults—who come to church school and go home. This may or may not be a large group. It may also include a few children dropped off for Sunday school and picked up afterward by an aunt or a grandmother or parent. These are three-hour people.

Group 2 includes the people who go to both church school and worship; they are four-and-a-half-hour people.

Group 3 is composed of the people who come to worship and then go home; they are three-hour people.

Figure 9.1 Church School, followed by Worship

9:30   Church School   1. ___

                      2. ___

11:00   Worship   3. ___

Group 1. Persons who are in church school and then go home
Group 2. Persons who are in both church school and worship
Group 3. Persons who are in worship and then go home

**Figure 9.2 Worship, followed by Church School,
        followed by Worship**

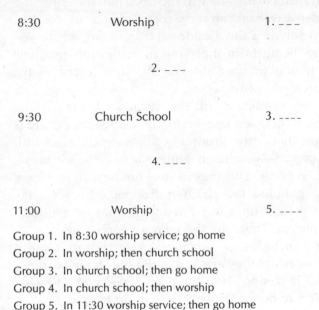

8:30	Worship	1. _ _ _
		2. _ _ _
9:30	Church School	3. _ _ _ _
		4. _ _ _
11:00	Worship	5. _ _ _ _

Group 1. In 8:30 worship service; go home
Group 2. In worship; then church school
Group 3. In church school; then go home
Group 4. In church school; then worship
Group 5. In 11:30 worship service; then go home

As shown in figure 9.2, the church that offers worship followed by church school followed by another opportunity for worship is, in fact, helping five groupings of people. Group 1 includes the people who come to the 8:30 worship service and go home; they are three-hour people. Group 2 consists of the people who go to worship and then to church school; they are four-and-a-half-hour people.

Group 3 consists of the people who come to church school and then go home; they are three-hour people. Group 4 includes those who go to church school and then to worship; they are four-and-a-half-hour people. Group 5 comprises the people who come to the 11:00 worship service and then go home; they are three-hour people.

It's important to note that when you have church school followed by worship and then decide to offer a new service of worship at 8:30, you move from helping three groupings to helping five groupings of people.

As shown in figure 9.3, when a church offers both worship and church school twice on Sunday morning, they are helping eight groupings of people. Group 1 consists of the people who come to the 9:30 worship service and go home.

Figure 9.3 Worship and Church School, Worship and Church School

9:30   1. ___ Worship   2. ___ Church School   3. ___

            4. ___   5. ___

11:00   6. ___ Worship   7. ___ Church School   8. ___

Group 1. In 9:30 worship; go home
Group 2. Parents in 9:30 worship, children in church school; then go home
Group 3. In church school at 9:30; then go home
Group 4. In worship at 9:30; then church school at 11:00
Group 5. In church school at 9:30; then worship at 11:00
Group 6. In 11:00 worship service; go home
Group 7. Parents in 11:00 worship, children in church school; then go home
Group 8. In church school at 11:00; go home

Group 2 is made up of the parents who are in worship at 9:30 while their young children are in church school at the same time. Group 3 comprises the persons who are in church school at 9:30 and then go home.

Group 4 is made up of the persons who are in worship at 9:30 and then go to church school at 11:00. Group 5 consists of those who are in church school at 9:30 and worship at 11:00.

Those in group 6 come to the 11:00 worship service and then return home. Group 7 includes parents who are in worship at 11:00 while their children are in church school at the same time. Group 8 consists of persons who are in church school at 11:00 and then return home.

By using these examples to help you do your own analysis, you'll be in a solid position to come to some conclusions about the groupings you can help in the future. As best you can, set aside your own preferences, habits, and conveniences.

Look at it through the eyes of the people you hope to help. In fact talk with some of them to discover what will help them as they worship God. The more possibilities you offer, the more people you will help.

10 :

The Comfortably Filled Sanctuary

YOUR SANCTUARY'S SEATING RANGE

The reciprocal dynamic of services and sanctuary contributes to the vitality of worship. We have considered services. Let's look at the sanctuary, or worship space. Among the six factors related to the services and the sanctuary, this is the fifth one to consider. It's not the first or the most important. It's simply one of six.

During services of worship, we find the seating range of the facilities to be perceived as one of the following:

- Uncomfortably crowded
- Comfortably filled
- Comfortably empty
- Uncomfortably empty

Most people prefer a worship space that is comfortably filled to uncomfortably crowded. Most people prefer not to worship in a facility that is comfortably empty to uncomfortably empty.

A worship service in a facility that is uncomfortably empty can feel hollow and lonely to many people, sometimes even depressing. In a worship facility that is comfortably filled to uncomfortably crowded, people feel that the worship is more dynamic. The sense of the presence of the people gives power and movement to the service.

Several elements contribute to a sanctuary's being perceived in the comfortably filled range:

- A large vestibule
- A wide center aisle or aisles
- Wide side aisles
- Short pews
- Generous legroom between pews
- A spacious chancel

A large vestibule gives an immediate sense of spaciousness to people who are entering. The wide center and side aisles help people have a sense of openness and comfort as they move to their pews. These also contribute to the sense of spaciousness as people cluster together to visit with one another after the service.

Short pews can seat up to eight people. These are more desirable than longer pews. Many people arrive early in order to secure aisle seats. Indeed, the aisle seats always go first.

People arriving later will need to step past those seated on the aisle. They will sit toward the center of a short pew, but they don't like to have to climb over four or five persons to reach the center of a longer pew. They feel trapped in the middle of a long pew.

In sanctuaries where the pews have been placed too close together, thereby limiting the room needed for people to scoot by others' knees in an effort to get to their seats, you can almost write off the middle of each pew. Sure, people will sit there on Easter or Christmas—and you won't see them back again until next Easter or Christmas.

It does no good to ask those with aisle seats to slide toward the middle to make room for latecomers. These persons came early so they could get their aisle seats, and their attitude is, "If they want to sit on the aisle, let them take the trouble to come early like I did." Try to have the pews spaced generously apart so there is room for latecomers to step in without knocking knees.

When calculating the actual seating capacity of your sanctuary, allow twenty-two inches per person. Some churches estimate seating capacity using sixteen inches. It's not simply a matter of bottom to bottom; it's also shoulder to shoulder. And in our time, the more reasonable measurement is twenty-two inches shoulder to shoulder. (To give you a comparison, on some airlines coach seating measures eighteen inches per seat; first-class seating is twenty-two inches.)

Measure each pew's length, divide by twenty-two inches, and you will have the number of people who can sit shoulder to shoulder in that pew. This formula will help you discover the real maximum seating capacity of your sanctuary.

The more spacious and open the chancel and the more cubic footage of space in the sanctuary—the higher the ceiling—the easier it is for people to thrive in a facility that is uncomfortably crowded. Conversely, when people see a crowded and cluttered chancel, they will tend to feel crowded and closed in. The lower the ceiling (which factors into cubic footage), the more cramped people will feel.

RURAL CHURCHES

In rural areas, a sanctuary is comfortably filled when 60 percent of the seating capacity is filled. There are two appropriate reasons for this. I call them (1) elbow room and (2) Mrs. Smith.

A person's decision to live in a rural area has much to do with elbow room. People live five to fifty acres apart by choice. They count on elbow room in day-to-day life, and when they come to church on Sunday morning, they count on their fair share of elbow room as well.

One family tends to sit on one end of the pew, and another family on the other aisle end of that same pew, and it's as if there were five to fifty acres between. That pew feels comfortably filled. And it is.

The second reason: Mrs. Smith. Mrs. Smith always sits "one in" on the third pew from the back on the left-hand side. Those who have worshiped together there these many years can still see Mr. Smith sitting there on the aisle, his elbow propped on the end of the pew. That is why she sits one place in—so he can have the aisle seat.

We can still see Mr. Smith sitting there, even though he died ten years ago of a heart attack. We can also still see Johnny Smith sitting beside his mom, even though Johnny is now called John and is married with three children and lives in Seattle. We can still see Nancy sitting there, too, even though Nancy is finishing a graduate degree at a nearby university.

When a new couple comes in and sits down "on top of them," we sort of wince. Can't they see that pew is already filled? The point is that when we look at the Smith family pew, we still see all four persons who sat there for many years. To Mrs. Smith—and to all the rest of us—that pew is already comfortably filled.

A city pastor might come to that rural church and look out on Sunday morning and think, "This sanctuary is forty percent empty," when, as a matter of fact, it is comfortably filled. In a rural church that can seat one hundred persons shoulder to shoulder, an average worship attendance of sixty means the sanctuary is comfortably filled.

CITY CHURCHES

In a city, 80 percent of capacity is comfortably filled. A pew that can seat ten is comfortably filled when eight people are there. When the ninth person shows up, they reluctantly move over. When the tenth person shows up, they wonder why they're being picked on. Why can't those others go sit somewhere else?

So in the city think 80 percent. A city worship facility that seats 400 shoulder to shoulder will be comfortably filled when 320 persons are there.

In both cases, rural and city, the comfortably filled principle holds true—60 percent and 80 percent, respectively, assuming you have a large vestibule, a wide center aisle or aisles, wide side aisles, short pews, pews spaced generously apart, a spacious chancel, and a high ceiling. When these are lacking, the 60 percent and 80 percent figures must be appropriately reduced.

ACTUAL COMFORTABLY FILLED SEATING CAPACITY

The following steps will help you to discover the actual comfortably filled seating capacity of your sanctuary. One reason I have researched the formula is that many congregations are unrealistic about their actual seating capacity. They were given some figure years ago that has been passed down without thoughtful study.

1. Main floor seating capacity
   at 22″ per seat   _____
   Omit front pews unless a railing
   is present
2. Choir seating capacity   _____

3. Balcony seating
   consider line of sight   _____
   frequently count 50 percent of total
4. Overflow and transept seating
   consider line of sight   _____
   frequently count 50–75 percent
   of total
5. Total gross seating capacity (add 1–4)   _____
6. Gross comfortably filled capacity   _____
   in rural area, 60 percent of number 5
   in city area, 80 percent of number 5
7. Reduce figure in number 6 by 4 percent
   for each of the following (a–f) that is
   lacking
   a. large vestibule
   b. wide center aisle or aisles
   c. wide side aisles
   d. short pews (seating eight or fewer)
   e. generous legroom between pews
   f. spacious chancel
   Actual comfortably filled seating capacity   _____

Once you know the actual comfortably filled seating capacity of your worship facility, you are in an excellent position to know whether—given your current worship attendance—your worship facility is

	Rural	City
Uncomfortably crowded	60%+	80%+
Comfortably filled	60%	80%
Comfortably empty	40%	60%
Uncomfortably empty	20%	40%

Once you know where the worship attendance and seating range are, you are in a solid position to grow forward.

UNCOMFORTABLY CROWDED, COMFORTABLY FILLED

When your services of worship are comfortably filled to uncomfortably crowded, there are five possibilities available to you:

- Deliver three of the first four central characteristics and adequate parking.
- Add major community Sundays.
- Add new worship services.
- Expand the size of sanctuary.
- Build a new sanctuary.

The first possibility is to deliver three of the first four central characteristics of a strong, healthy, effective church, and adequate parking. See my book *Twelve Keys to an Effective Church* for resources on these and for the formula on adequate parking. The first four central characteristics are

1. Specific, concrete missional objectives
2. Pastoral and lay visitation in the community
3. Corporate, dynamic worship
4. Significant relational groupings

Deliver any three of these four in outstanding ways, as well as the tenth central characteristic—adequate parking—and you can thrive in an uncomfortably crowded sanctuary.

The second possibility is to add major community Sundays. These are discussed in depth in my book *Effective Church Finances*, and I commend to you that chapter in the book. Major community Sundays are essentially of the same strength and scope as Christmas and Easter services. By adding eight major community Sundays, in addition to Christmas and Easter, we have major worship services ten times during the year rather than only twice. When you offer the high-quality major community Sundays that I have in mind, people will not only put up with an uncomfortably crowded church, they will thrive on and benefit from it.

The third possibility is to add new services of worship at other times. A new service is planned and developed primarily to benefit those we're not yet reaching and helping; as it does this it will also help some of the people who are seeking relief from being uncomfortably crowded in our present services. Chapter 11 of this book describes the simplest, best way to begin a new service of worship.

A helpful rule of thumb is this: Don't divide services of worship. If a service is uncomfortably crowded, and you're delivering three of the first four central characteristics and adequate parking, leave it alone. That congregation will be fine.

I would suggest diligently pursuing the first three avenues—developing the central characteristics of an effective church, scheduling major community Sundays, and adding new services—before you even consider either of the next two, which are expanding the present facilities or building new facilities.

As a consultant for many years, I've had considerable experience with both the expansion of sanctuaries and the building of new sanctuaries. Speaking from such wide experience, I strongly suggest that you leave these as options of last resort. You can constructively deal with being uncomfortably crowded by seeking solutions in the first three possibilities. I would use all three before I expanded the present facilities or built new ones.

WHAT TO DO WHEN THE SANCTUARY IS UNCOMFORTABLY EMPTY

In many congregations the sanctuary seating ranges from comfortably empty to uncomfortably empty. In fact, this is a more widespread pattern than uncomfortably crowded. There are six ways to help your church improve on its uncomfortably empty situation:

- Deliver three of the first four and the tenth central characteristics of an effective church.
- Add major community Sundays.
- Reconsider the time of the service(s).
- Add new services of worship.
- Fill the chancel area.
- Respace the pews.

When the seating is comfortably empty to uncomfortably empty, we are probably not delivering three of the first four central characteristics of an effective church. It is quite likely that we also have inadequate parking.

Now, the solution is not as simple as simply providing more parking; there are churches that have adequate parking and are still empty on Sunday morning. It is a matter of looking at which three of the first four central characteristics we can grow and develop, advance and improve. Then we need also to be certain we have adequate parking. In these ways we can grow our comfortably empty or uncomfortably empty sanctuary toward being comfortably filled.

The second possibility is to add major community Sundays. One of the best ways forward is to have ten major community Sundays a year. At least then, on those major community Sundays, the sanctuary may be more nearly comfortably filled. That will help.

A third way to build up an uncomfortably empty church may involve taking a close look at the time of the service. You may decide to move the eleven o'clock service to ten o'clock or to nine o'clock. Your church may have established a time for the service years ago, and perhaps in your particular area that time no longer works. It may have worked well at one time, but no longer.

And, fourth, as ironic and incongruous as it may seem, even when the service of worship is comfortably empty to uncomfortably empty sometimes the best thing we can do is to add a new worship service at another time. Regrettably, too many congregations think they should fill their present service of worship before they add a new one.

As a matter of fact, if the people we might reach and help could come to an eleven o'clock service, they probably would have done so by now—there's plenty of room, there's adequate parking. For whatever reason, that worship time is not convenient for them.

Sometimes, regrettably, what we would like is new people to help fill our service of worship, whereas the real task for us is to help them worship God. If we discover persons in the community who are more likely to worship at 8:30 on Sunday morning or 4:00 on Saturday afternoon, or at any other convenient time, we can help them by providing an opportunity at that time, so that they can worship God.

Whether or not that helps us enhance attendance at our present comfortably empty or uncomfortably empty eleven o'clock service is beside the point. We are not in this endeavor just to fill up a service of worship at a time familiar and convenient to us. We are in this endeavor to help people with their life and destiny in the name of Christ. And, frequently, one of the best ways to do this is to add a new service.

Another option is to fill up the chancel area—to grow the choir. The more filled the chancel, the more filled the sanctuary. The emptier the sanctuary, the more important it is to fill the chancel. When you have a sanctuary that is uncomfortably empty, it is even more important to build a choir that fills the chancel.

People who look forward and see a chancel that is full of people have the sense that the whole sanctuary is fuller. Sitting in an uncomfortably empty sanctuary and seeing an uncomfortably empty chancel gives people a double sense of emptiness. Sometimes the solution is to develop a large choir and fill the chancel.

The sixth, and last, possibility to consider is to respace the pews. One sanctuary had 15 pews on each side of a center aisle. Each pew was long enough to seat 10 persons, which potentially meant 150 could sit on each side, for a total of 300. However, the pews were spaced so close together that no one could pass. The middle three seats in each pew would typically be vacant. That throws away 45 seats on each side. The aisle seats were filled, with usually about three people on one end and four on the other. The pew was "full" with seven people. This really meant that each side could accommodate 105 persons, for a total of 210.

We took out three rows of pews on each side and respaced them so that there was ample room to get from the aisle to the center of each pew without knocking knees. By doing this we actually increased the total seating capacity from 210 to 240. We now had 12 pews on each side, each of which could realistically seat 10 people, with the middle of the pew easily accessible.

The respacing of the pews did another thing. It helped the sanctuary look less uncomfortably empty. By respacing the pews, we actually increased the realistic seating capacity and helped change the appearance from uncomfortably empty to comfortably empty.

Try the first five possibilities before you even consider going to the sixth option. Once you have worked on the first five, you might not need to respace the pews.

Note that among these six possibilities you don't find any suggestion of merging services. The rule of thumb is,

Don't merge services. In consulting with one congregation that offered two Sunday morning services, I learned they were planning to vote in two weeks on whether to have just one service.

At 8:30 they averaged 80 people. At 11:00 they averaged 120 people. Their sanctuary was uncomfortably empty at both services. Some thought that by merging and having only one service, the sanctuary would be close to comfortably filled.

I told them I was puzzled as to why they were voting. The vote would come out exactly the way it had been coming out every Sunday for the past five years. Eighty people would vote for two services, and 120 people would vote for one service. Majority wins—they would end up with one service. But two years from now they would be lucky if their worship attendance was 90–110; it would never reach 200 simply by merging.

It was not accidental that the 80 people who were coming to the 8:30 service attended then. There was plenty of room for them at 11:00. The reason they came at 8:30 was that, for them, 8:30 was the convenient time.

Someone said, "Wouldn't it be wonderful if we could all worship together, as one family? Wouldn't there be a kind of epiphany in that?" For the most part, the people who campaign for merging services attend the 11:00 service and hope that the 8:30 people will join them at that time. I hardly ever hear the 11:00 people saying what a marvelous epiphany it would be if we could all worship together at 8:30.

My point is simply this: When you merge two worship services, you seldom end up with one strong service. Instead you will end up losing people you have already been reaching. It doesn't show up immediately. But over a two-year period, the people will simply come less frequently.

Fortunately, when the sanctuary is uncomfortably crowded to comfortably filled, you have five excellent possibilities. And fortunately, when the sanctuary is comfortably empty to uncomfortably empty, you have six excellent ways forward. With wisdom and prayer, select the possibilities that will work best for you and your mission.

PUTTING SANCTUARY SEATING IN THE PROPER PERSPECTIVE

I began researching the consideration of sanctuaries and seating range in the 1960s and have continued to study this pattern across the years with thousands of congregations since then. It is helpful for you to know these conclusions:

- Seating range is only one of many factors to consider as you strengthen your congregation's mission; it is not the most important one.
- A few persons have made too much of this seating factor; their overemphasis has distracted congregations from developing the primary components that help worship services to be corporate and dynamic
- The seating range factor was of more importance in a churched culture; it has less value in a mission field.

Twelve central characteristics contribute to a congregation's strength and effectiveness. They are found in table 10.1.

You will find out more about these twelve central characteristics in my book *Twelve Keys to an Effective Church*. Congregations are strong, healthy, and effective when they deliver nine out of these twelve. Focus primarily on the nine you can best deliver, and don't become preoccupied with seating range.

**Table 10.1 The Central Characteristics
of Successful Churches**

Relational Characteristics

1. Specific, Concrete Missional Objectives
   1   2   3   4   5   6   7   8   9   10

2. Pastoral/Lay Visitation in Community
   1   2   3   4   5   6   7   8   9   10

3. Corporate, Dynamic Worship
   1   2   3   4   5   6   7   8   9   10

4. Significant Relational Groups
   1   2   3   4   5   6   7   8   9   10

5. Strong Leadership Resources
   1   2   3   4   5   6   7   8   9   10

6. Solid, Participatory Decision Making
   1   2   3   4   5   6   7   8   9   10

Functional Characteristics

7. Several Competent Programs and Activities
   1   2   3   4   5   6   7   8   9   10

8. Open Accessibility
   1   2   3   4   5   6   7   8   9   10

9. High Visibility
   1   2   3   4   5   6   7   8   9   10

10. Adequate Parking
    1   2   3   4   5   6   7   8   9   10

11. Adequate Space and Facilities
    1   2   3   4   5   6   7   8   9   10

12. Solid Financial Resources
    1   2   3   4   5   6   7   8   9   10

More specifically, when considering the seating range factor, know this: Congregations that deliver three out of the first four central characteristics and the tenth one—adequate parking—will have happy, thriving, uncomfortably crowded worship facilities, and no one particularly notices the uncomfortably crowded seating range. Indeed, the congregations flourish.

When persons are helped with a specific human hurt and hope in mission, when they have been shepherded in visitation, when the worship service is corporate and dynamic, when they have found their significant relational grouping—indeed, when they have found fulfillment in any three of these four—and there is adequate parking, they will put up with, and actually thrive in, a worship facility that is uncomfortably crowded.

A brief word on parking. People are more likely to put up with an uncomfortably crowded worship facility when there is adequate parking. Church leaders make a poor choice when they focus on the seating range of the worship space but continue to have inadequate parking. You make an excellent choice when you have adequate parking and uncomfortably crowded worship facilities. That is a better relationship.

Focusing too much on the less significant factor of seating range has distracted many congregations from developing the primary components that will strengthen their worship services. Congregational worship is shared and dynamic, stirring and inspiring, helpful and hopeful when

- the service is warm and winsome
- the music is dynamic and inspiring
- the service has power and movement
- the services and sanctuary help the congregation reach persons in the community in mission

• the preaching expresses the character of the gospel and the quality of compassion

These are the five major components of strong, healthy services of worship. Whenever these are richly and fully present, the worship life of a congregation thrives.

Keep the seating range factor in its rightful and proper place. Indeed, if one did deliver the worship attendance for a comfortably filled sanctuary and did *not* deliver the major components of worship, the sanctuary would soon be uncomfortably empty.

In our time few congregations have the problem of being uncomfortably crowded. Their dilemma is that their worship facility is uncomfortably empty. To focus on a comfortably filled principle is of little help to them. Their best future is to focus on which nine of the twelve central characteristics they plan to grow forward.

The seating range factor was truer in a churched culture and has less value in a mission field. Today, thriving, healthy congregations are busy with the mission. They are delivering nine of the twelve central characteristics. They don't rely on social conformity to bring people to them as it did in a churched culture. They are purposeful about reaching persons in their community. They share help, hope, and home.

When it was a churched culture, people had their own pew and their own parking space. Indeed, they had filed deeds at the nearby county courthouse on both. Some people still do this, and some still retain their original deed.

At the same time, given the desperate, urgent, extraordinary dynamics of our time, the factor of seating range pales into insignificance. Most people who have caught the spirit of mission know this. We have been given one of the richest ages for mission the planet has ever seen. In strong, healthy congregations the mission is central.

When you consider the reciprocal dynamic of the services and the sanctuary, consider all six factors:

- The number of worship service options you offer
- The convenience of the options you offer
- The options that help "three-hour" persons
- The groupings you reach and help
- The realistic seating range of your sanctuary
- The new worship services you offer

Develop four of the six, choosing those that will best enhance the vitality of your worship services.

11 :

Developing
a New Service

We begin a new service of worship as our gift to the community. We do not try to get people to church to help us with our agenda, our institution and its survival. We set aside any preoccupations in that direction.

The community has been good to our church. We are seeking to do something with and for people in the community. We share this new service of worship as a gift, freely given, to be helpful in the lives of people in our community.

Developing a new worship service is very much like growing a new congregation. There are four steps:

1. Discover the mission groupings

2. Do informal development

3. Develop the music

4. Advance the worship leadership

MISSION GROUPINGS

The first step in developing a new service is to discover the grouping or groupings of persons with whom you hope to be in mission in your community. Adding a new service offers you the opportunity to reach a whole grouping of persons you're not now reaching.

It is less helpful to add a new service of worship simply to accommodate the overflow from a service that has become uncomfortably crowded. Were you to focus only on that, you would likely shortcut the steps helpful to reach a new grouping or groupings of persons, and you would thereby throw away an opportunity to reach and help new persons in your community. If some persons currently attending an uncomfortably crowded service of worship also decide to become a part of the new service, that is a plus.

Consider the community that your congregation, as a mission outpost, seeks to serve. Within that community, identify one or more significant groupings of persons with whom you hope to be helpful. Think through your own gifts, strengths, and competencies as a congregation to be genuinely helpful. Then select a mission team of five to eight persons to provide leadership in reaching out to and helping with one of the groupings in the community you have selected.

INFORMAL DEVELOPMENT

The best way to add a new service is to have a three- to five-month period of informal development. You don't add a new service by simply running an announcement in the church bulletin or newsletter saying that three weeks from now there will be a new worship service at a certain time. Such a service will start weak.

Start strong and grow stronger. There's no need to start weak and then try to make a weak service into a strong one. That's a hard road to travel. Live with this conviction: Our first worship service will be strong, and we will grow it even stronger.

In order to start strong, look forward to an informal development period of three to five months. While the following figures are merely suggestive and will vary greatly from one congregation and community to the next, the basic pattern of informal development is consistent.

The originating mission team of five to eight persons discovers thirty to forty persons who look forward to being part of the new service of worship that will begin during a specific week three to five months from now. I encourage you to study my book *Visiting in an Age of Mission* for specific suggestions on both the groupings and the ways your mission team can reach out to them in your community.

For the moment, let me simply mention that this mission team can reach out to some of the following groupings:

- Recent first-time worshipers
- Newcomers in the community
- Occasional worshipers
- Constituent families in specific stages of life
- Persons served in mission
- Persons in their own relational networks
- Persons in the relational networks of the congregation
- Persons in a specific vocational grouping
- Persons in a specific neighborhood
- Inactives in the congregation

Visiting in an Age of Mission describes these groupings more fully and suggests ways to reach them and the best timing to be in contact with them.

When the team invites someone to be part of the new worship service, the invitation is shared in this spirit:

> *We invite you to be a beginning participant in our new worship service.*
>
> *It is specifically designed to be helpful to families with children.*
>
> *It will begin the second week in October.*
>
> *The current leadership team is* _____
> _____.
>
> *These are some of the persons who are looking forward to being part of the new service.* (Illustrate some of the families who are involved and who may be known by the person you are inviting.)

The invitation is to be a "beginning participant," not a founding member. It's more like a date than a marriage. We hope it will grow to be a long-term relationship.

The new service, in its focus, purpose, and resources, will directly benefit the individual and their family. Create a spirit of expectancy and creativity. This will be a most helpful service of worship in the lives of the people who participate. It will be a simple, stirring, inspiring service. The people who participate will discover resources directly helpful to their lives.

Over a short, concentrated period of time, perhaps six weeks, the five- to eight-person mission team grows itself into a grouping of thirty to forty persons looking forward to the new service of worship. It's a good idea to gather this initial grouping of thirty to forty persons for a get-together of fun, good times, and sharing to become more fully acquainted.

From among this group select another five- to eight-person mission team to grow yet another thirty to forty persons who are looking forward to the new worship service.

This second mission team will invest six to eight weeks in reaching out to persons in the community. All of the others in the first group of thirty to forty are reaching out as well.

At the same time, this second mission team is reaching out in intentional, intensified ways. It too can have a fun get-together to become more fully acquainted.

Select from the second grouping of thirty to forty persons another mission team to reach a third grouping of thirty to forty persons in the community. This team's work will likely be done in the weeks just prior to the launching of the new service of worship. In this way, three major groupings will come together to launch the first service of worship.

When a worship service is begun by gathering one grouping only, that grouping quickly becomes a "single cell." Frequently they see the new service as their private service, and it's difficult to grow the attendance at the new service beyond that limited grouping.

When a service begins with a core of two groupings, that often sets the stage for a two-cell church fight. The best thing a two-cell congregation does is fight. One group tries to claim the power and authority of "old-timers" and treats the other cell as "newcomers," and the fight is on.

When you take the time and effort to begin a new service with three groupings, over the long run you increase the chances that the service will be genuinely helpful with more persons in the community. It will mean 90 to 120-plus persons will gather to worship God in that first service. To be sure, three groupings will sometimes still fight, and three groupings will take turns. And you will have launched a strong service of worship.

From the initial three groupings develop a leadership team to plan the strengths and the convenient time for the new service of worship. We know the week we plan to begin the new service. As we discover the range of people who look forward to being beginning participants, they will help decide the most convenient time for the new service to be held. This leadership team, in consultation with the three initial groupings, develops the major components of the new service. The strength of the leadership team lends mutual trust, respect, integrity, credibility, and confidence to the new service. This will be among the best worship services in the community. Using *Dynamic Worship*, the team will think through ways to make the new service corporate and dynamic, stirring and inspiring, helpful and hopeful. The leadership team will focus on the specific ways to achieve the following goals:

- The service is warm and winsome.
- The music is dynamic and inspiring.
- The service has power and movement.
- The service and sanctuary help the congregation reach persons in the community in mission.
- The preaching expresses the character of the gospel and the quality of compassion.

The leadership team helps the five major components of a strong, healthy service of worship to be well in place—present in the first service and growing further.

Please note this well: The figures will vary from one congregation to the next. On occasion a congregation might intentionally launch a new service of worship that will be, by design, a strong, small service. Not every service has to be large. At the same time, the art is to start strong and to grow stronger. Given the size of the space in which you plan to worship, begin the first service comfortably empty to comfortably filled. The art is not to start uncomfortably empty—to start weak—and then try to grow.

Remember that old saying, "If you don't have time to do it well the first time, when will you find time to fix it?" Yes, we're sometimes too prone to quick closure. Worship is so precious to people's life and destiny. Worship is so sacred and vital to life. Take enough time in the beginning to do it well. With a new service of worship, start strong with the first service and grow even stronger with each service from then on.

At some point prior to the beginning of the new service, the team can invite the beginning participants to a good times gathering to share fellowship together, and to give people the chance to express some of their own hopes for the new worship service.

The team can share follow-up notes of thanks and appreciation for the good, fun fellowship and for the excellent ideas and suggestions that emerged from the gathering.

The team can share personal notes, phone calls, and letters, as appropriate, keeping everyone up to date on the developing plans for the service, encouraging them to look forward to the service, and inviting their prayers and suggestions for the service. This is especially helpful in the two months prior to beginning the new service.

DEVELOPING THE MUSIC

As you grow the initial three groupings for the new service, it is important to develop music that suits the mission groupings you hope to help. The aim is for the new service of worship to have its own unique strengths in music. Look at the eleven possibilities for music discussed in part 2. Select the six that will be central to this new service.

For example, the new service could have its own choir or other music group. There might be a choir director and pianist or some other kind of music leaders. As your three mission teams build the three initial groupings, some 90 to 120-plus persons, the choir director, the pianist, and a core music team can begin to emerge.

The emerging music team, in consultation with the leadership team, plans and develops fitting music—dynamic and inspiring—for the new service. There is no need to ask an eleven o'clock choir to cover this new service of worship also.

Each worship service has its own integrity, identity, sustainability, and reliability. No service should depend on the resources of another service of worship. The emerging music team, the choir director, and the pianist (or organist—it depends on the nature of the music and the nature of the service) begin building the choir for the new service. That is part of their leadership contribution.

I grant you that growing a new choir is hard work. It's even harder to expect one choir to cover two services. That is grossly unfair to the original choir that is doing well at its service, just as it is unfair to the participants in the new service. Among them there are a number of people who—given half a chance—would look forward to participating in a new choir for the new service.

The choir director for this new service, with the help of the pianist, the music team, the leadership of the congregation, and the pastor, can focus on developing a new choir from among these groupings:

- The initial three groupings for the new service

- The primary groupings of persons in the community with which this new service plans to be in mission

- His or her own relational networks in the community

- The music networks in the community

- Educational, civic and community, and recreation networks in the community

- Unchurched young couples and single parents with small children in the community

- Unchurched early retired people in the community
- Constituent participants in the congregation
- Unchurched persons who have a relationship—acquaintances, work associates, friends, family—with the 90 to 120 originating participants in the new service
- The shepherding networks of the congregation

The music team, the choir director, and the pianist function as a mission team. They don't wait for someone else to deliver choir members to them. They seek people out. They develop a choir as part of the mission. A choir developed in this spirit becomes a mission choir.

Consider the music networks in the community as important resources. The new choir director will bring his or her own network of relationships among the music community. When you select a genuinely competent choir director for the new service, that person will bring three to five to ten persons who will look forward to being a part of the new choir.

Constituent participants are those who are currently involved in some program or activity within the congregation but are not currently active in a service of worship. It may very well be that singing in the new choir will become their entry point into worship participation.

The shepherding network includes all those who have been helped in some shepherding way during this past year by your congregation and who are not now actively participating in a service of worship. Feel free to invite them to be part of the choir and to be part of this new service of worship.

When you start a new choir for a new service of worship, you are in fact starting a new significant relational grouping. The choir ultimately becomes like a family, and many people proceed on their life's pilgrimage supported by the belonging and sharing they find in their choir family.

In one sense, when you start a new choir for a new service of worship, it's like starting a new adult Sunday school class but without needing to find a new classroom. They will work well with whatever rehearsal space is available to them and will be at home in the new service of worship as they share their best music.

A New Choir Director

When you add a new service, add a new choir director. In most congregations, the existing choir director is either part-time or volunteer. The new service will gather at a different time, possibly a different day of the week. It would be most unfair to ask the part-time or volunteer person, who is doing excellent work at the eleven o'clock service on Sunday, to take responsibility for the music in the new service as well. Affirm the good work that person is doing, and select another person for the new music responsibilities.

When you have a part-time choir director for your present service, feel free to bring on board a new part-time choir director when you add a new service. That person will be in the best position to grow strong music with its own integrity for the new service. The music will be chosen to reach the groups of persons whose life and destiny you seek to help through the new service.

Some people may be concerned about the costs and what effect a new service will have on finances. A few may worry that we cannot afford to add a new music position. Some may worry that all the energies invested in starting the new service might be better invested in just getting out there and getting more members; usually there is an underlying expectation that simply adding more members will bolster the giving. Actually it is more accurate to say that giving grows in relation to increased attendance, not increased membership.

Let's use an example of a church with an average worship attendance of 200 and total giving of $200,000. This church starts a new worship service following the steps we have discussed. They do it well. They start strong and grow stronger.

They will soon reach, in the first or second year, an average worship attendance nearing 150 to 200 in the new service. The first few times it may be 90 to 120. Given strong mission, reasonable time, and a full music program, average attendance at that new service will steadily increase.

When it is well developed in the beginning, the new service can grow to be as strong as your present service. The new service will then deliver net new giving equal to the giving in your present service. It is usually safe to count on the new service eventually to contribute $200,000 of net new giving.

The formula works like this: Divide your current total giving by your current average worship attendance (for example, $200,000 divided by 200). The result is a ratio of worship attendance to giving (in the example, one worship participant to $1,000).

Using the example, this doesn't mean that there are 200 people, each giving $1,000. An average worship attendance of 200 really represents 250 to 300 people. Some come every Sunday, some come twice a month, some come once a month, some come Christmas and Easter. It takes 250 to 300 people to create an average worship attendance of 200. And it takes those same 250 to 300 people to generate the total giving of $200,000.

A new service of worship, as it grows its way to an average attendance of 200, will reach a new pool of 250 to 300 people. Whatever the increase in average worship attendance is—assume that it's 100 in the beginning—multiply that by the dollar figure in your ratio of attendance to giving. The resulting figure will serve as a predictor of the net new giving that will grow from the new worship service.

When attendance in the new service reaches an average of 100, you can predict giving, based on the example, of approximately $100,000. And as attendance at the new service grows closer to 150 to 200 people, giving will be closer to $150,000 to $200,000.

Keep in mind that there is no correlation between membership growth and giving growth. The correlation is between worship attendance growth and giving growth. In many churches the membership grows, but the worship attendance reaches a plateau, and the giving reaches a plateau. When the giving reaches a plateau, you will almost always find that the worship attendance has reached a plateau.

When you launch a new service of worship, you launch a new source of giving. It is perfectly reasonable to invest money in a new part-time choir director and a pianist (or an instrumental group or any of the eleven possibilities already discussed) who will develop the music for this service of worship.

The funds you invest will be a wise investment. The new giving that will come from those attending this new worship service will more than cover the initial investment. The puzzle is not the money for the new part-time choir director. The key puzzle is finding an excellent choir director, pianist, and/or instrumental group who will have fun building both the choir and the new service of worship in ways that will be meaningful to those you hope to reach in mission. Finding these persons is what takes wisdom. The money will come.

ADVANCING THE WORSHIP LEADERSHIP

The fourth step in adding a new worship service is to advance the worship leadership. Grow the leadership for the new service from among the initial groupings of 90 to 120 new persons. From these new persons you will discover your new-person greeters, ushers, and worship leaders.

From among these persons you can build all the components of the worship service needed to help it be among the best, most helpful services of worship in the community.

It is not helpful to ask the people serving during the eleven o'clock service to be leaders at the new service. Calling on them to be new-person greeters, ushers, and worship leaders for the new service has these consequences:

- It pulls them away from the good work they already enjoy doing at their regular eleven o'clock service.

- Their contribution at the new service suffers from a divided loyalty. They feel that they're "real" ushers at the eleven o'clock service and just "helping out" at the new service.

- New persons will be blocked from the opportunity to serve as new-person greeters, ushers, pew greeters, and worship leaders.

You grow the worship leadership for the new service from among the people who will be served and helped in this new service. This means the new service will have its own strengths and will not seem like a stepchild of the original worship service. It will sustain itself and enhance the mission of your congregation in the community.

Start *new* services of worship. Don't invest your time in splitting or merging services. Developing a new worship service is like growing a new congregation. Discover the mission groupings. Do informal development. Develop the music. Build the worship leadership.

New services reach new people. The primary reason for starting a new service is to reach people you're not now reaching. Do it well, and God will bless your mission.

12:

The Power of the Spirit

MISSION GROWTH

I invite you to be a participant and a leader in the Mission Growth Movement. The empowerment of the Spirit is felt in the growth of the mission. We are focusing on growing the mission more than growing the membership. We do not ignore the effort at membership growth, but that is not our primary focus.

Movements reveal their primary priorities in the way they keep their statistics of success. Their inherent theology of the church is revealed in their theology of statistics. Congregations focusing on the growth of the mission keep their statistics in the following priority:

1. Persons served in mission
2. Persons who have discovered Christ
3. Visitation in the community
4. Average worship attendance
5. Average participation in significant relational groupings
6. New groupings started

7. Total giving to all causes
8. Giving to mission and service
9. Membership

"Persons served in mission" is the number of people in the community directly helped by the congregation during the year. These persons are neither members nor constituents of the congregation. They are *directly* helped. This is not "third-party" helping through a food or clothing bank located elsewhere. This is not a landlord-tenant relationship where a group simply uses the church's facilities. The persons are helped with a specific human hurt and hope, and they directly link the helping with the congregation.

"Persons who have discovered Christ" is the number of those who have grown in their pilgrimage and discovered Christ as their Savior and Lord during the year. "Visitation in the community" is the number of persons, nonmembers and nonconstituents, with whom the congregation has visited in the community. The other statistical items are familiar. And while sometimes a given congregation or denomination may keep additional statistics, the list I've just offered makes the priorities clear.

Regrettably, some people turn this sequence of priorities upside down and focus primarily on membership growth. In the Mission Growth Movement the primary priorities have to do with mission, new Christians, visitation, worship, and groupings. Giving and membership follow these.

THE DEMISE OF SOCIAL CONFORMITY

We have this good news:

- The day of social conformity is over.
- The day of mission growth has come.

The movement of the future is the Mission Growth Movement. Many people throughout the world are active participants and leaders in growing the mission. Social conformity has seen its day. We don't worship in order to conform to social expectation. We worship to discover God's purpose for our life and for the empowerment of the Spirit for mission.

In August of 1991 I contributed—along with several other prominent specialists—to an event focused on the question "Where is the Christian church headed in the twenty-first century?"

A point made by Peter Drucker at that conference is helpful here. He postulated two reasons for the decline of religion:

- The decline in social conformity
- The increase in freedom of choice

He speculated that the decline in religion was more a decline in social conformity. There was a time when social conformity delivered persons to the church. It was a time when people who wanted to borrow money at the nearby bank to buy a house filled out a loan application that asked for the name of their pastor and two other references. When someone missed church on a Sunday morning, it was taken as a sign of severe illness or perhaps death. Such was the pressure of social conformity.

At the time of the founding of this country, some colonies let people stay only if they were members of the dominant sect of the colony. Those who were not members had two choices: join or leave.

In the great population migrations of the 1800s and following World War I and World War II, the religious groupings that migrated tended to take along a pattern of social conformity. Peter Drucker's first point was that we no longer experience such pressures to conform.

His second point was that we are experiencing an increase in freedom of choice. I can remember hearing people say, "Every time the doors of the church were open, we were there." As I have reflected on this, I've come to see that one of the primary reasons we were there every time the doors of the church were open was because church was about the only thing in town; it had the only open doors. There was not much else to do. Church was the primary option available.

Now we have many options to choose from. Church is no longer the only activity in town. The increase in freedom of choice is phenomenal. Peter Drucker's wise conclusion is that we're not, therefore, dealing primarily with a decline in religion. We're dealing with the combined impact of a decline in social conformity and an increase in freedom of choice.

I've thought about these two points for some time, and I'd like to advance the discussion in this way. I think it is more precise to say that we're dealing with a decline in *church*, not a decline in *religion*. There is no decline in religion. Many studies confirm that people's interest in religion and things of the spirit is soaring.

People in our time have a profound interest in religion. The problem is that this interest in religion is not connecting with the institutional church. The decline is not in religion; it is in church.

I think there are four reasons for this decline—the two mentioned previously plus two more. The decline in church is because of

- the decline in social conformity
- the increase in freedom of choice
- the increase in new forms of social conformity that do not include church
- the lingering of customs, habits, and traditions of a churched culture that no longer work on a mission field

We can confess to God that we have counted on social conformity too much to deliver people to us. We have waited on them to find us. One has to ask whether social conformity is a solid way to build the mission.

We can give thanks to God for the decline in social conformity. With the decline in social conformity we are more likely to seek people out. We are more likely to share mission and evangelism in the community. We are more likely to do what Christ has invited us to do.

Don't long for a return of social conformity. In times of social conformity the church is never at its best. In such times the church becomes bloated and bureaucratic, lazy and indifferent. The church is at its blazing best in a mission field.

We wouldn't want to put ourselves in the position of advocating a decrease in freedom of choice. We are a people who believe in freedom of choice. And the more choices available, the more likely the church is to be at its best. The fewer the choices available, the easier it is for the church to settle for mediocrity. The number of choices pushes us to share the mission at our best.

The third reason for the decline in church is the increase in new forms of social conformity that do not include church. Social conformity has not gone away. It is still with us. But it no longer includes church. It does include a wide range of informal and formal social, vocational, recreational, political, and community groups.

Now, we might invest much time in challenging the new forms of social conformity that have emerged. And it is important that we do some of that work. At the same time, we can best look to our own house.

The fourth reason for the decline of church is the foremost reason—namely, the lingering of customs, habits, and traditions of a churched culture that no longer work in a mission field. We can confess to God that we have spent too much time and energy trying to be successful with behavior patterns that worked in a churched culture and no longer work now. Here is one helpful definition of insanity: Insanity is continuing to repeat the same patterns of behavior and expecting to get different results.

We can confess to God that we have done this too much. We have assumed that if we were more committed and worked harder, the things that worked in the churched culture of the 1940s and 1950s would work in the present and the future. And it is not happening.

We need to let go of some of the behavior patterns of the past. We need to discover new ways to advance the mission in this time. We need to give up some of the older ways. They're not working, and they haven't been working for more than twenty years. My book *Effective Church Leadership* contains many suggestions about which lingering customs, habits, and traditions we can give up and offers new ways to lead that will help us in an age of mission. Know this well: The day of social conformity is over. The day of mission growth has come.

MISSION GROWTH AS RENDERING SERVICE IN THE NAME OF CHRIST

God invites us to grow the mission. God invites us to help persons with their life and destiny in the name of Christ. The movement of the future is the Mission Growth Movement. Recall that the purpose of worship is not to get new members or to achieve church growth, but to discover God's purpose for our life and to empower the Spirit for mission.

The lead question of the Mission Growth Movement is, Who are we helping in the name of Christ?

The question is not, Do we want to grow more members? or Do we want to help the institution survive and grow?

The focus of the question is on mission for the integrity of mission—mission for the sake of mission. The focus is not on mission to get more members. The focus is on the number of persons we serve in mission in a given year, not the number of members we get. It's interesting to note that declining denominations focus on the number of members lost and gained in a given year.

Mission movements keep their first statistics on persons served in mission. They track first the number of persons who have been helped during the past year. Then they track the number of persons who have discovered Christ during the past year. They develop objectives for these. Their interest is in the persons they serve in mission and those who discover Christ. Congregations in the Mission Growth Movement keep their priorities straight.

To paraphrase Paul in 1 Corinthians 13:11,

> *When I was a child, I did childish things.*
> *And when I became an adult, I gave up childish ways.*

When we were children, we counted on social conformity to deliver people to our churches. We waited on them to find us.

When we became adults, we put away childish things, and we focused on how we could be in mission. We focused on who we could help with their life and destiny. We do the mission and it leads us to worship. There we discover God's purpose for us and the empowerment of the Spirit.

Cast Your Nets. You Will See Jesus.

In the Gospel of John, chapter 21:1–8, we discover the Stranger standing on the shore. The disciples do not know it is Jesus. He asks the disciples,

"Have you caught any fish?"

The answer comes back, "No."

The disciples had been out fishing all night long. Following the resurrection, they had not known what to do next. Peter had said, "I guess I'll go back to fishing." Some of the disciples had said, "We'll go with you. We don't know what to do either." Old ways die hard.

But as the night wore on, they began to discover that not even the old ways worked anymore. They used to be pretty good fishermen. They tried all the old favorite fishing places where in years past they had always caught fish.

Nothing. Early that morning they are headed to shore. Their boat is empty of fish and they are filled with despair.

The Stranger on the shore invites them, "Cast your nets on the right side of the boat."

And they did. The first miracle is that they did. We sometimes think that the miracle is that their nets were now so loaded with fish that they could not bring them into the boat. That is the second miracle. The first miracle is that they did. They could have rowed the other way. They could have held a committee meeting. They could have said, "That won't work." The miracle is that they did. We do discover new ways.

And yes, the second miracle is that now the nets were loaded with fish. New ways do work.

The third miracle is in the words, "It is Jesus." Until they cast their nets he had been the Stranger on the shore. Now, after having cast their nets, they discover that the Stranger is the Christ. Peter gathers himself up, throws himself into the sea, and rushes to the shore. And the other disciples hurry in the boat to Christ.

It is in casting our nets that we discover Christ. It is not that we discover Christ and then cast our nets. It is not that we worship and then go and do the mission.

In sharing the mission, we discover Christ. In Mark 16:7 the instruction is given to tell the disciples to go to Galilee, and that there they will find Christ. The instruction is not to stay in an Upper Room, or to visit a synagogue, or to hold a committee meeting. They are encouraged to go to the mission field. That is where they will find him. It is as we share the mission that we find Christ.

As we discover Christ in the mission, we are led to worship. Worship grows out of mission. And, as we worship, we discover strengths, insights, resources, confidence, and assurance for the mission.

On a mission field times are not "normal." This is no longer the pleasant safety of a churched culture. Life is more desperate, chaotic, confusing. Mission and worship are more urgent and decisive. Mission, grace, praise, and power become more crucial for our lives and for the world.

To be sure, as we worship we discover the mission. But it is not so much a deductive relationship wherein we worship first and then go and do mission as it is a reciprocal relationship. As we live life, as we share mission, we discover Christ and are led to worship, and as we worship we are led to healthy, whole lives in mission.

MISSION AND POWER

Wherever worship is corporate and dynamic, stirring and inspiring, helpful and hopeful, these four are present:

- Mission
- Grace
- Praise
- Power

We worship to gain strength for the mission. We worship to discover grace amid the sinfulness of our lives. We worship to praise God as the source of our being and our future. We worship to discern the power of the Spirit with which to live rich, full Christian lives in mission.

Some services of worship disenfranchise people, cause them to feel yet more defeated and powerless. Those are not services of worship; they are services of abject servitude. Some services are dull and poorly led. Some services of worship are a wasted hour or, at best, a quiet nap.

Worship is mission. The purpose of worship is to help persons discover the mission to which God is calling them and the power to live that mission in the world. It is as we worship God, as we hear the gospel preached, and as we share the sacraments that we discover the mission to which God is calling us.

Our worship is helpful, healthy, and effective when

• the mission is richly and compassionately shared,
• the worship is corporate and dynamic,
• the gospel is helpfully and rightfully preached, and
• the sacraments are fully shared.

The church is not at its best when it concentrates on only the last three. Those three are inside-the-church practices. But when the whole service has about it the spirit of mission, it helps the church to be in the world, and when that happens the worship, the preaching, and the sacraments have a dynamic of mission about them.

Worship is grace. Worship is the breath of God. When we worship, we feel God's grace surrounding us, permeating our life—our very being. We discover a sense of peace, confidence, and assurance. We know that our sins are forgiven and that we are made new through the grace of God.

We experience the sense that God is with us, and we are with God. Our anxieties and troubles take their rightful and proper perspective. We receive the grace of encouragement and hope. We see both in the moment and beyond the moment that the grace of God continues to lead us toward that future that God has promised and prepared for us.

Worship is praise. We worship to praise God, not because God needs our praise. We would be arrogant to assume that. But in our praise of God, we discover who we are and whose we are. And as we make that discovery, we find that we are God's mission people. It is through our praise of God that God helps us discover the mission God has prepared for us.

Worship is power. We worship to discover power for the week to come. We don't worship so much in relation to the week or months or years that have passed. We worship to launch the week ahead, to have a sense of confidence, hope, and inspiration for the days before us. We worship to discover power in our own life and destiny so that we can live fully in God's mission.

God invites us to live lives of mission, grace, praise, and power. This is a mission field. This is an age of mission. The church's worship has always been at its best in a mission field, whether in the first century or the twenty-first century. In a churched culture, the worship is bland and boring, stifling and stuffy, indifferent and "inside." It is in a mission field that the church discovers worship as mission, grace, praise, and power. This is where the church's worship is at its best.

God invites our best in life, in mission, in worship. To be sure, God receives our worst and forgives. God constantly invites our best and calls us to forward the mission.

With joy, wisdom, and prayer select the major components of worship, the possibilities for worship, that will best advance and strengthen the mission and the worship of your congregation. The peace of God, the compassion of Christ, and the power of the Spirit be with you.

About the Author

Kennon L. Callahan is the most sought after speaker, author, and consultant with congregations and denominations in the country. Combining his background as a pastor and theologian with extensive experience as a speaker, researcher, and consultant, he has worked with thousands of congregations of all sizes and denominations over the past thirty-six years. He has spoken extensively in the United States, Canada, Australia, and New Zealand and has worked with denominational leaders from Korea, Africa, the Caribbean, and South America.

Dr. Callahan is highly regarded for his thoughtful, creative, and dynamic leadership of seminars that take advantage of his planning expertise, motivational speaking, and solid, theological perspective. He brings this in-depth perspective to the areas of long-range planning, effective visitation, dynamic worship, leadership, time management, multiple staff development, stewardship, and financial planning.

Building upon his original book, *Twelve Keys to an Effective Church*, Dr. Callahan has written *Twelve Keys: The Leaders' Guide*, which provides additional resources and principles for pastors and leaders. *Twelve Keys: The Planning Workbook* helps planning committees and local congregations develop their most effective long-range plan step-by-step. *Twelve Keys: The Study Guide* shares key principles and biblical references to assist groups in their use of the Twelve Keys program. *Effective Church Leadership* shows pastors and key leaders how to apply effectiveness principles to the day-to-day leadership of the local church. *Giving and Stewardship* is written for everyone in the congregation. *Effective Church Finances* is helpful to pastors, administrators, finance committees, and other key leaders. *Visiting in an Age of Mission* offers ways to reach out beyond the church to the surrounding community. This body of *Twelve Keys* literature is widely used worldwide and has been translated into a number of languages.

Dr. Callahan has served congregations in Ohio, Texas, and Georgia—in rural and urban settings. For twelve years he helped build Lovers Lane Methodist Church in Dallas, Texas, into one of the largest Methodist congregations in the world, first as Minister of Evangelism and more recently as Minister of Finance and Administration.

Having earned the B.A., M.Div., and S.T.M. degrees, Dr. Callahan went on to earn his Ph.D. in systematic theology. He has taught on the faculty of Candler School of Theology, Emory University, from 1972 to 1982. He continues to teach there, leading advanced seminars several times a year. Dr. Callahan is the founder of the National Institute for Church Planning and Consultation, based in Dallas, Texas. The Institute provides seminars for and consultations with local congregations and denominations to advance the effectiveness of pastors and congregations in the mission of the church.